**You Can Make in 5 Minutes**

# 152
# NON-SAD
## LUNCHES

YUM!

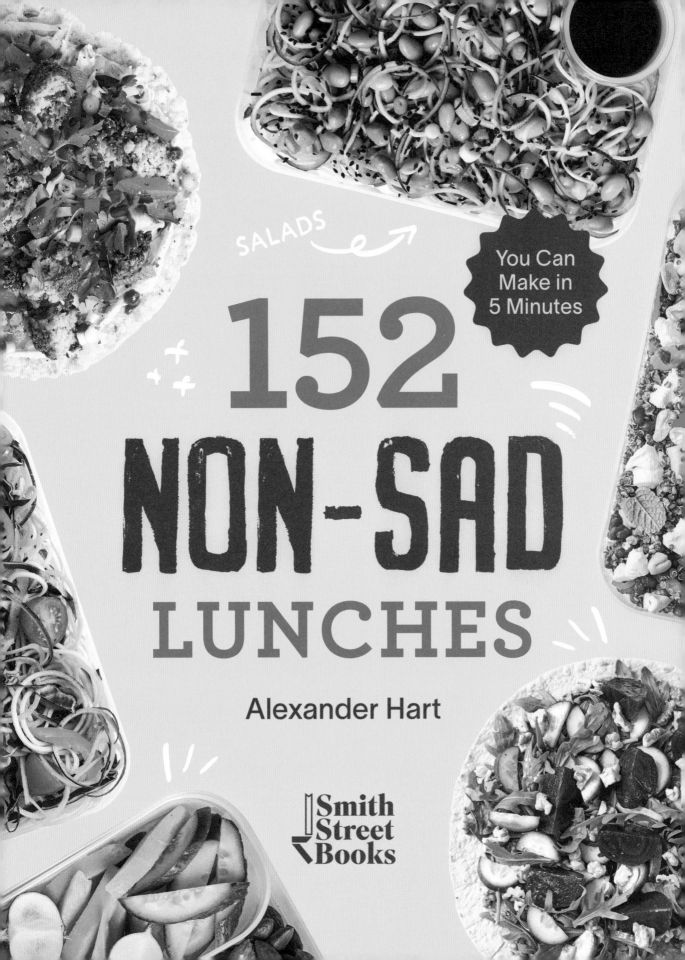

SALADS

You Can Make in 5 Minutes

# 152

# NON-SAD

# LUNCHES

Alexander Hart

Smith
Street
Books

Contents

# Introduction

During a busy working week, it can be hard to make the time for a delicious, nutritious lunch. And thus, the sad desk lunch was born: a hastily thrown-together soggy sandwich or something greasy and brown from the work cafeteria mindlessley consumed at your desk while working through what was meant to be your lunch break.

Help is here! These speedy salads are designed to be made in the morning before you start work and will remain crisp and fresh until lunchtime. Keeping the dressing separate is the key to maintaining a fresh crunchiness. Soggy salads are not your friend, so find yourself a lunchbox with a dedicated dressing container or use a small jar.

Using the 152 recipes in this book, you will be equipped with so many lunch options you'll never run out of ideas. Most of the salads can be made from scratch in 5 minutes, while others make the most of repurposing last night's leftovers into a healthy and delicious lunch. Either way, these simple salads will be better tasting and more nutritious than your nearest takeaway lunch option.

Even better, this book is loaded with low-carb and wholegrain recipes (with heaps of vegetarian and vegan options) that are built around a central protein and lots of fresh produce, so you'll be returning to your desk feeling satisfied and revitalised.

The chapters that follow separate the recipes into six handy categories: Classics and New Classics, Noodles and Zoodles, Grains and Seeds, Beans and Legumes, Bento Boxes, and Wraps. When your well of lunch-inspiration has run dry, just flick to your favourite genre of salad and find something to prepare for tomorrow. If you've found a salad that really tickles your fancy, double or triple the quantities in the recipe and eat it throughout the week. You'll be thanking yourself each day.

There's one last thing. Whenever possible, try and step away from your desk for lunch. Even if you have something delicious to eat, lunch at your desk is still a bit sad. There is one energy boost that no salad can ever provide: a change of scene. Maybe you only have 20 minutes to spare, but take that time to step away from your desk and find yourself a spot that feels quiet and comfortable. Make your lunch break a moment of respite, not just another task to juggle between emails. It is a break, after all.

# Salad ingredients

Here are a few notes on some of the ingredients used in this book, along with tips and tricks to help cut down your prep time even further.

### BEANS & LENTILS
Although the recipes in this book call for tinned beans and lentils – as they're a speedy option for adding to salads and wraps – you can, of course, soak and cook your own beans and lentils ahead of time and store them in the fridge. One of the major advantages to this is that you avoid the salt and sugar of the brine that most tinned varieties are stored in.

### BEETROOT
Cooked beetroot (beets) are available from the supermarket, usually found in vacuum-sealed packets, tins or jars. Mix it up and use golden or striped beetroot when they're in season.

### CHEESE
Good-quality hard cheeses, such as parmesan and pecorino, can be purchased shaved, grated or shredded, and crumbled feta is available in tubs in the refrigerated section of your supermarket.

### COOKED CHICKEN
Shredded cooked chicken is available in most supermarket delis. Alternatively, buy or cook a whole roast chicken, chop or shred the meat yourself and store in an airtight container in the fridge for up to 4 days. Another healthy option (if you have time) is to poach some chicken breasts for use throughout the week.

### CORN
Some of the recipes call for tinned sweet corn; however, if you have more time, chargrill a fresh corn cob instead. Slice off the kernels and add to your lunchbox with the remaining salad ingredients. Alternatively, you can cook the corn ahead of time and keep the kernels in an airtight container in the fridge for up to 3 days.

### DAIRY ALTERNATIVES
There are now so many vegan dairy alternatives that the options can seem daunting. Always check the labels and as a general rule, the fewer ingredients listed, the better the product. Look out for hidden sugar and salt too!

## DRESSINGS

For most of the recipes in this book, the dressing is kept separately so you can dress your salad just before you eat it. You can save yourself some more time in the morning by mixing your dressing the night before and keeping the container in the fridge – you could even prep a whole week's worth in advance.

## GRAINS & NOODLES

### Bulgur

The recipes in this book allow bulgur to soak and 'cook' in the time between preparing your salad in the morning and eating it at lunchtime. If you have time to prepare it the night before (and you'd rather not take an extra jar with you), make the bulgur according to the packet instructions and store in an airtight container in the fridge for up to 4 days.

### Instant (ramen) noodles

Check the packet instructions, but these should cook in boiling water in 2–3 minutes. Rinse under cold water and drain.

### Quinoa & brown rice

There are various 'quick' and 'instant' quinoa and brown rice products that are ready in 2–3 minutes. Cook according to the packet instructions and allow to cool. Alternatively, if you have time to prep regular quinoa or brown rice ahead of time, cook a large batch according to the packet instructions, then cool and store in an airtight container in the fridge for up to 4 days. Even easier, make enough for leftovers when cooking quinoa or brown rice for dinner, then toss with the remaining salad ingredients in the morning. If you can, try using a combination of black, red and white varieties of quinoa to mix things up a little.

### Soba noodles

Cook according to the packet instructions. Rinse well under cold water and drain.

### Vermicelli noodles

To prepare vermicelli noodles, place in a bowl, cover with boiling water and allow to sit for 3–4 minutes, giving them a bit of a stir occasionally to loosen them. Rinse under cold water and drain.

## HARD-BOILED EGGS

Make a batch ahead of time and keep in the fridge for up to 1 week. To cook, place your eggs in a saucepan and cover with cold water. Bring to the boil over medium–high heat, then cover, remove from the heat and set aside for 8–11 minutes (depending on how hard-boiled you like them). Drain, cool in iced water and peel just before adding to your salad.

## HERBS

To save extra time, chop all of your fresh herbs together.

## MINCED GARLIC & GINGER

Available in jars – or tubes (usually sold as 'paste') – from the supermarket, these really are a time-saving wonder. Alternatively, you can make your own: blitz a large quantity of garlic or fresh ginger in your food processor with a little water, salt and a drop of olive oil. It will keep well in an airtight container in the fridge for up to 2 weeks, or press flat in a zip-lock bag and store in the freezer for up to 2 months.

## NUTRITIONAL YEAST

Some of the recipes call for nutritional yeast, sometimes sold as yeast seasoning, which is a vegan ingredient that not only adds a delicious umami flavour to dishes, but also packs in an impressive list of vitamins and minerals. It can be used in many ways, but is often seen as the vegan equivalent of parmesan cheese.

## POMEGRANATE

The recipes call for frozen pomegranate seeds for the sake of convenience, but you can definitely use fresh seeds if you have them. To save some prep time, remove the seeds from the pomegranate and store in an airtight container in the fridge for up to 3 days.

## PRE-CUT VEGETABLES

Supermarkets carry a large range of packaged pre-cut vegetables that keep really well in your fridge, which is what we recommend using to keep your prep time to around 5 minutes. Look out for broccoli or cauliflower 'rice'; shredded carrot, cabbage and lettuce; spiralised zucchini / courgette (zoodles) and beetroot (beets); and other convenient combination products, such as coleslaw and mixed salad leaves.

## ROAST BEEF

Purchase sliced roast beef from your supermarket deli, or use leftovers if you have them.

## TOASTED NUTS & SEEDS

Toast nuts and seeds ahead of time, leave to cool completely, then store them in an airtight container in your pantry for up to 1 month.

## VEGAN MAYONNAISE

Vegan mayonnaise is easy to find in most supermarkets. There are many different types with different flavour profiles – so find the right one for you. Of course, if you have the time, making your own isn't too difficult – many use a base of aquafaba, which is the brine left over from a tin of chickpeas.

## WRAPS

There are many different types of wraps available – some wheat-based, some gluten-free, some flavoured and coloured with natural ingredients including beetroot (beet), spinach and tomato. Feel free to use whatever you like for those wrap recipes.

## NOTES ON QUANTITIES

We find you rarely need exact quantities when putting together a salad, so we've used 'handfuls of' in many cases, making ingredients quick to throw in. Feel free to adjust the quantities to make use of what you might already have in your fridge.

All tablespoons are 15 ml / 3 teaspoons.

assics &
assics & New
assics & Ne
lassics & Ne
lassics & Ne
lassics & N
Classics & N
Classics & N
Classics &

New Classics
New Classics
New Classics
New Classics
New Classics
New Classics
New Classics
New Classics

# Baby beetroot, walnut & ricotta salad

1 Spoon the ricotta into a small, airtight container.

2 Toss the remaining salad ingredients together, then tip into your lunchbox.

3 Combine the dressing ingredients in a small jar or container with a tight-fitting lid. Season to taste.

4 Pour the dressing over the salad just before eating and toss well. Dot the ricotta over the top.

50 g (1¾ oz) ricotta

2 large handfuls of baby spinach leaves

200 g (7 oz) cooked baby beetroot (beets), quartered

¼ red onion, thinly sliced

50 g (1¾ oz) toasted walnuts, roughly chopped

Date dressing
- 1 medjool date, pitted and finely chopped
- 2 teaspoons honey
- 1 tablespoon white wine vinegar
- 2 tablespoons extra virgin olive oil

The nutty earthiness of baby beetroot is perfect in this salad, but you can use any roast veggies here. Look for good-quality fresh ricotta, or use goat's curd or Persian feta instead.

Classics & New Classics

# Broccoli rice salad with buttermilk dressing

1   Toss the salad ingredients together, then tip into your lunchbox.

2   Combine the dressing ingredients in a small jar or container with a tight-fitting lid. Season to taste.

3   Pour the dressing over the salad just before eating and toss well.

½ head of broccoli, blitzed to coarse grains

handful of shredded carrot

2 tablespoons dried cranberries

¼ red onion, thinly sliced

3 tablespoons slivered almonds

¼ red bell pepper (capsicum), diced

handful of rocket (arugula)

Buttermilk dressing
- 2 tablespoons buttermilk
- 1 tablespoon Greek yoghurt
- juice of ½ lemon
- ¼ teaspoon minced garlic

To make this recipe super fast, use pre-cut broccoli and carrots, and use a good-quality store-bought buttermilk ranch dressing, or make the dressing a day ahead.

# Fennel & radicchio citrus salad

1   Segment the orange over a bowl to catch the juice. Combine the segments with the juice and the fennel and toss gently.

2   Toss through the remaining salad ingredients, then tip into your lunchbox.

3   Combine the dressing ingredients in a small jar or container with a tight-fitting lid. Season to taste.

4   Pour the dressing over the salad just before eating and toss well.

1 orange or blood orange

½ small fennel, shaved

¼ small radicchio, shaved

handful of pitted kalamata olives

50 g (1¾ oz) toasted walnuts, roughly chopped

¼ red onion, thinly sliced

handful of parsley, chopped

Citrus dressing
–   juice of ½ orange
–   2 teaspoons red wine vinegar
–   1 teaspoon honey
–   1 teaspoon dijon mustard
–   2 tablespoons extra virgin olive oil

16

This is a fantastic winter salad, try using blood oranges when they are in season. You can save some time by cutting the orange and fennel the night before.

Classics & New Classics

# Bibimbap salad with kimchi dressing

1   Spread the cabbage over the base of your lunchbox and top with the other salad ingredients.

2   Combine the dressing ingredients in a small jar or container with a tight-fitting lid.

3   Pour the dressing over the salad just before eating and toss well.

100 g (3½ oz) shredded cabbage

1 tablespoon toasted sesame seeds

1 hard-boiled egg, cut into wedges

large handful of shredded carrot

small handful of bean sprouts

1 short cucumber, diced

1 spring (green) onion, sliced

Kimchi dressing
-   30 g (1 oz) kimchi, roughly chopped
-   1 teaspoon caster (superfine) sugar
-   1 tablespoon rice wine vinegar
-   1 teaspoon sesame oil
-   1½ tablespoons neutral-flavoured oil

This recipe uses shredded cabbage as the base for a lighter take on the Korean rice-bowl classic. The kimchi dressing gives this salad a real kick – feel free to increase the quantity if you like it hot.

# Brussels sprouts with hazelnuts, pear & pecorino

1 Toss the salad ingredients together, then tip into your lunchbox.

2 Combine the dressing ingredients in a small jar or container with a tight-fitting lid. Season to taste.

3 Pour the dressing over the salad just before eating and toss well.

150 g (5½ oz) brussels sprouts, shredded

2 tablespoons dried cranberries

1 pear, thinly sliced

30 g (⅓ cup) grated pecorino

30 g (1 oz) roasted hazelnuts, roughly chopped

small handful of parsley, chopped

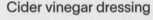

Cider vinegar dressing
- 2 teaspoons dijon mustard
- 1 teaspoon honey
- 1½ tablespoons apple cider vinegar
- 2 tablespoons extra virgin olive oil

The sweetness from the pear and dried cranberries (also known as craisins) are the perfect foil for the peppery bite of the raw sprouts. Apple will work just as well as pear and walnuts are great here, too.

# Left-over roast vegetable salad

1 Toss the salad ingredients together, then tip into your lunchbox.

2 Combine the dressing ingredients with 1 tablespoon of water in a small jar or container with a tight-fitting lid. Season to taste.

3 Pour the dressing over the salad just before eating and toss well.

200 g (7 oz) left-over roast vegetables, sliced or cut into bite-sized pieces

small handful of parsley, roughly chopped

2 large handfuls of baby spinach leaves

30 g (1 oz) cashew nuts, roughly chopped

2 teaspoons sumac

Tahini dressing
- 1 teaspoon minced garlic
- 2 tablespoons tahini
- juice of ½ lemon

When I'm cooking roast veggies for dinner, I always make sure I cook extra for leftovers to use in my lunch the next day. Substitute toasted pine nuts or almonds if you don't have cashews.

Classics & New Classics

# Som tum

1 For the dressing, pound the chilli and garlic using a mortar and pestle, add the dried shrimp and peanuts and pound until you have a rough paste. Stir in the palm sugar, fish sauce and lime juice.

2 Toss the papaya, beans and tomatoes together, mix through the dressing, then tip into your lunchbox. Pop some lime wedges on top to squeeze over just before eating.

½ small green papaya, shredded

3 snake (yard-long) beans, chopped into 2 cm (¾ in) lengths

large handful of grape (baby plum) tomatoes, halved

2 lime wedges

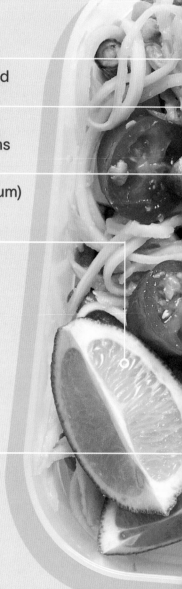

Som tum dressing
– 2 red bird's eye chillies (deseeded if you prefer less heat)
– 2 garlic cloves
– 1 tablespoon dried shrimp
– 1½ tablespoons roasted unsalted peanuts
– 1 tablespoon grated palm sugar
– 2 tablespoons fish sauce
– juice of 1 lime

A Thai staple, som tum is fresh and big on flavour. Adjust the chilli depending on how hot you like it. If you want a really quick option, look for pre-made som tum dressing at your local Asian grocer.

Classics & New Classics

# Spring vegetable salad with ricotta

1 Combine the zest, ricotta and a pinch of salt in a small, airtight container.

2 Blanch the asparagus and peas in boiling salted water for 2 minutes. Drain and refresh under cold running water. Tip into your lunchbox and mix in the remaining ingredients.

3 Combine the dressing ingredients in a small jar or container with a tight-fitting lid. Season to taste.

4 Pour the dressing over the salad just before eating and toss well. Dot the lemony ricotta over the top.

zest of ½ lemon

50 g (1¾ oz) ricotta

½ bunch baby asparagus, halved

60 g (2 oz) shelled fresh peas

large handful of snow peas (mangetout), halved lengthways

large handful of sugar snap peas

small handful of mint leaves

Honey–mustard dressing
- juice of 1 lemon
- 1 teaspoon dijon mustard
- 1 teaspoon honey
- 2 tablespoons extra virgin olive oil

This salad is best made in spring when asparagus and peas are crunchy and sweet. If the peas are really fresh, you can leave them raw. Use quality ricotta, as you want it to be lovely and creamy.

Classics & New Classics

# Shredded beetroot, dill & mustard seed salad

1 Toss the salad ingredients together, then tip into your lunchbox.

2 Combine the dressing ingredients in a small jar or container with a tight-fitting lid. Season to taste.

3 Pour the dressing over the salad just before eating and toss well.

200 g (7 oz) shredded raw beetroot (beet)

2 tablespoons mustard seeds, toasted

large handful of mixed salad leaves

large handful of dill, roughly chopped

Lemon dressing
- juice of ½ lemon
- 2 tablespoons extra virgin olive oil

You can buy pre-shredded beetroot from the supermarket to save on your prep time. Feel free to use a mix of different leaves, including rocket (arugula), sorrel and baby spinach.

Classics & New Classics

# Raw cauliflower tabbouleh

1  Toss the salad ingredients together, then tip into your lunchbox.

2  Combine the dressing ingredients in a small jar or container with a tight-fitting lid. Season to taste.

3  Pour the dressing over the salad just before eating and toss well.

¼ head of cauliflower, blitzed to coarse grains or use store-bought cauliflower 'rice'

2 spring (green) onions, sliced

1 short cucumber, diced

handful each of dill, mint and parsley, roughly chopped

handful of grape (baby plum) tomatoes, quartered

Lemon dressing
–  juice of ½ lemon
–  2 tablespoons extra virgin olive oil

This is a low-carb take on tabbouleh, replacing the traditional bulgur wheat with blitzed cauliflower. This salad makes a great accompaniment to grilled vegetables or meats with a dollop of hummus.

Classics & New Classics

# Caprese salad

1 Toss the salad ingredients together, then tip into your lunchbox.

2 Combine the dressing ingredients in a small jar or container with a tight-fitting lid. Season to taste.

3 Pour the dressing over the salad just before eating and toss well.

1 buffalo mozzarella ball, roughly torn

large handful of basil leaves, roughly torn

large handful of mixed red and yellow grape (baby plum) tomatoes

large handful of rocket (arugula)

Balsamic dressing
- 1 tablespoon balsamic vinegar
- 2 tablespoons extra virgin olive oil

Treat yourself to some good-quality fresh buffalo mozzarella for this salad or, for a simpler option, use a few bocconcini balls instead.

33

Classics & New Classics

# The new Greek salad

1   Toss the salad ingredients together, then tip into your lunchbox.

2   Combine the dressing ingredients in a small jar or container with a tight-fitting lid. Season to taste.

3   Pour the dressing over the salad just before eating and toss well.

large handful of grape (baby plum) tomatoes

handful of pitted Kalamata olives

50 g (⅓ cup) crumbled feta

1 short cucumber, diced

¼ yellow bell pepper (capsicum), diced

¼ red onion, thinly sliced

1 teaspoon dried oregano

Greek dressing
-   1 tablespoon white wine vinegar
-   2 tablespoons extra virgin olive oil

A classic combination of flavours that's hard to beat. When tomatoes are in season, try replacing the grape tomatoes with some heirloom varieties.

# Chicken fattoush with tahini yoghurt

1 Lightly brush the pita bread with olive oil, sprinkle with sumac, then quickly toast until golden. Set aside to cool, then break into pieces and place in a small, airtight container.

2 Toss the remaining salad ingredients together, then tip into your lunchbox.

3 Combine the tahini yoghurt ingredients with 2 teaspoons of water in a small jar or container with a tight-fitting lid. Season to taste.

4 Pour the dressing over the salad and toss through the pita bread just before eating.

1 pita bread

olive oil, for brushing

sumac, for sprinkling

100 g (3½ oz) shredded cooked chicken

1 baby cos (romaine) lettuce, chopped

large handful of grape (baby plum) tomatoes, halved

small handful each of mint leaves and parsley, chopped

Tahini yoghurt
- 1 tablespoon lemon juice
- 1 tablespoon tahini
- 1 tablespoon Greek yoghurt
- 1 teaspoon honey

This salad is a great way to use up leftovers if you've made souvlakis or wraps for dinner the night before. Pita breads can be toasted ahead of time, broken up and kept in an airtight container.

Classics & New Classics

# Ploughman's salad

1  Toss the apple in the lemon juice. Add the remaining salad ingredients and toss together, then tip into your lunchbox.

2  Combine the dressing ingredients in a small jar or container with a tight-fitting lid. Season to taste.

3  Pour the dressing over the salad just before eating and toss well.

½ apple, thinly sliced

1 teaspoon lemon juice

50 g (1¾ oz) cheddar, cut into cubes

2 radishes, thinly sliced

1 celery stalk, sliced

4 cos (romaine) lettuce leaves, roughly chopped

handful of grape (baby plum) tomatoes, halved

6 pickled onions, halved

Hot mustard dressing
–  ½ teaspoon hot English mustard
–  1 tablespoon apple cider vinegar
–  2 tablespoons extra virgin olive oil

Find a nice sharp cheddar and good-quality pickled onions for this ingenious salad. Try substituting the cheddar for blue cheese and use pear instead of apple, for a twist on the classic.

Classics & New Classics

# Roast beef salad with smoked almonds

1 Place the almonds in a small, airtight container.

2 Toss the zucchini ribbons in the lemon juice. Add the remaining salad ingredients and toss together, then tip into your lunchbox.

3 Combine the dressing ingredients in a small jar or container with a tight-fitting lid. Season to taste.

4 Pour the dressing over the salad and toss through the almonds just before eating.

30 g (1 oz) smoked almonds, chopped

1 small zucchini (courgette), peeled into ribbons

1 teaspoon lemon juice

100 g (3½ oz) sliced roast beef, torn into pieces

large handful of grape (baby plum) tomatoes, halved

handful of parsley, chopped

Lemon & chilli dressing
- pinch of dried chilli flakes
- juice of ½ lemon
- 1 teaspoon dijon mustard
- 2 tablespoons extra virgin olive oil

If you can't buy smoked almonds you can just use plain roasted almonds. This recipe is great with roast beef from your deli, but even better made with leftovers from a Sunday roast.

Classics & New Classics

# Panzanella

1 Place the dressing ingredients in a small jar. Season to taste and mix well.

2 Toss the salad ingredients together. Drizzle with the dressing and toss to combine, then tip into your lunchbox.

50 g (1¾ oz) stale sourdough or other crusty bread, torn or cut into bite-sized pieces

1 small short cucumber, diced

¼ red onion, thinly sliced

100 g (3½ oz) mixed ripe tomatoes, chopped

handful of basil leaves, torn

Vinegar & garlic dressing
- 1½ tablespoons red wine vinegar
- ½ teaspoon minced garlic
- 2 tablespoons extra virgin olive oil

A classic Italian salad designed to avoid wasting stale bread. Dress this salad in the morning – or at least 30 minutes before eating – to give the bread some time to soak up all the delicious flavours.

Classics & New Classics

# Chicken taco salad

1 Place the tortilla chips in a small, airtight container.

2 Toss the avocado in the lime juice. Add the remaining salad ingredients, then tip into your lunchbox.

3 Combine the dressing ingredients in a small jar or container with a tight-fitting lid. Season to taste.

4 Pour the dressing over the salad just before eating and toss through the tortilla chips.

handful of tortilla chips, broken

½ avocado, diced

juice of ½ lime

large handful of grape (baby plum) tomatoes, halved

100 g (3½ oz) shredded cooked chicken

30 g (1 oz) queso fresco, crumbled

75 g (2¾ oz) drained tinned sweet corn kernels

small handful of coriander (cilantro), roughly chopped

Jalapeño crema dressing
- 1 tablespoon lime juice
- 1 tablespoon Greek yoghurt
- 3 slices pickled jalapeños, finely chopped

Queso fresco is a mild-flavoured Mexican cheese, available at Latin grocers and some good supermarkets. You can use any cheese you like, but mild feta is the closest substitute.

Classics & New Classics

# Vietnamese chicken coleslaw

1 Place the peanuts and shallots in a small, airtight container.

2 Toss the remaining salad ingredients together, then tip into your lunchbox.

3 Combine the dressing ingredients in a small jar or container with a tight-fitting lid.

4 Pour the dressing over the salad just before eating and toss through the peanuts and shallots.

1 tablespoon chopped peanuts

1 tablespoon crispy-fried shallots

100 g (3½ oz) shredded cooked chicken

handful of shredded carrot

small handful of bean sprouts

large handful of shredded white cabbage

small handful each of mint and coriander (cilantro) leaves, chopped

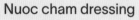

Nuoc cham dressing
- 1 tablespoon fish sauce
- 1½ tablespoons lime juice
- 2 teaspoons rice wine vinegar
- 1 teaspoon caster (superfine) sugar
- ½ red bird's eye chilli, deseeded and sliced
- ½ teaspoon minced garlic

Crispy-fried shallots are available in big packets at Asian grocers. They're fantastic to have on hand in your pantry, as they make a quick, crunchy addition to salads and noodle dishes.

Classics & New Classics

# Niçoise salad

1   Toss the beans, tuna, olives, onion, tomatoes and anchovy (if using) together, then tip into your lunchbox. Top with the hard-boiled egg.

2   Combine the dressing ingredients in a small jar or container with a tight-fitting lid.

3   Pour the dressing over the salad just before eating and toss well. Season to taste.

100 g (3½ oz) blanched green beans

95 g (3¼ oz) tin tuna in spring water

small handful of pitted kalamata olives

¼ red onion, thinly sliced

handful of grape (baby plum) tomatoes, halved

3 anchovy fillets, chopped (optional)

1 hard-boiled egg, halved

French dressing
- 1 tablespoon red wine vinegar
- 2 tablespoons extra virgin olive oil

To save yourself some time, hard-boil a few eggs at the start of the week, so you have them on hand for whipping up this quick salad. Hard-boiled eggs will keep in the fridge for up to a week.

Classics & New Classics

# Chinese silken tofu salad

1  Toss the salad ingredients together, then tip into your lunchbox.

2  Combine the dressing ingredients in a small jar or container with a tight-fitting lid.

3  Pour the dressing over the salad just before eating and toss well.

100 g (3½ oz) firm silken tofu, cut into cubes

1 short cucumber, chopped

large handful of grape (baby plum) tomatoes

1 spring (green) onion, chopped

handful of bean sprouts

small handful of coriander (cilantro) leaves, chopped

2 teaspoons toasted sesame seeds

Chilli soy dressing
–  ½ teaspoon each minced garlic and ginger
–  1 red bird's eye chilli, deseeded and chopped
–  1½ tablespoons light soy sauce
–  1 teaspoon sesame oil
–  1 tablespoon black vinegar
–  ½ teaspoon sugar

Silken tofu can be quite delicate. The 'soft' variety isn't suitable for a salad as it will fall apart, so look for 'firm' or 'extra-firm'. If you prefer some heat, leave the seeds in the chilli, or add some chilli oil.

Classics & New Classics

# Prosciutto, rocket & nectarine salad

1 Toss the nectarine in the lemon juice. Add the remaining salad ingredients and toss together, then tip into your lunchbox.

2 Combine the dressing ingredients in a small jar or container with a tight-fitting lid. Season to taste.

3 Pour the dressing over the salad just before eating and toss well.

1 ripe nectarine, sliced

1 teaspoon lemon juice

3 slices prosciutto, torn

30 g (1 oz) shaved parmesan

large handful of rocket (arugula)

Honey–dijon dressing
- 1 teaspoon dijon mustard
- 1 teaspoon honey
- juice of ½ lemon
- 2 tablespoons extra virgin olive oil

This salad is a summer treat when stone fruits are in season. It works just as well with peaches, too, and you can substitute fresh buffalo mozzarella for the parmesan for a more mellow flavour.

Classics & New Classics

# Prawn cocktail salad

1. Squeeze the lemon juice over the avocado and gently toss to combine. Toss through the remaining salad ingredients, then tip into your lunchbox.

2. Combine the dressing ingredients in a small jar or container with a tight-fitting lid.

3. Pour the dressing over the salad just before eating and toss well. Season to taste.

juice of ½ lemon

1 avocado, diced

150 g (5½ oz) cooked peeled prawns (shrimp)

handful of shredded iceberg lettuce

1 short cucumber, chopped

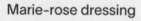

Marie-rose dressing
- 1½ tablespoons whole-egg mayonnaise
- 1 tablespoon tomato ketchup
- 1 tablespoon lemon juice
- dash of Tabasco sauce, to taste

Don't knock this deconstructed '80s classic until you've tried it. It's filling, nutritious and delicious!

Classics & New Classics

# Raw pad thai salad

1 Toss the salad ingredients together, then tip into your lunchbox.

2 Combine the dressing ingredients in a small jar or container with a tight-fitting lid.

3 Pour the dressing over the salad just before eating and toss well.

½ carrot, spiralised or grated

1 short cucumber, sliced

¼ red bell pepper (capsicum), thinly sliced

2 spring (green) onions, sliced

50 g (1¾ oz) snow peas (mangetout), trimmed and sliced

handful of bean sprouts

small handful of unsalted peanuts, roughly chopped

Tamarind dressing
- ½ teaspoon minced garlic
- ½ teaspoon minced ginger
- 1 tablespoon tamarind purée
- juice of ½ lime
- 2 teaspoons fish sauce
- 2 teaspoons caster (superfine) sugar

This recipe is a fantastic low-carb alternative to the beloved Thai dish. Save time by using pre-cut vegetables and a store-bought Thai-style dressing.

Classics & New Classics

# Chicken, mango & jalapeño salad

1 Toss the salad ingredients together, then tip into your lunchbox.

2 Combine the dressing ingredients in a small jar or container with a tight-fitting lid. Season to taste.

3 Pour the dressing over the salad just before eating and toss well.

½ ripe mango, diced

100 g (3½ oz) shredded cooked chicken

1 baby cos (romaine) lettuce, chopped

¼ red bell pepper (capsicum), diced

small handful of coriander (cilantro), roughly chopped

Jalapeño dressing
- juice of ½ lime
- 3 pickled jalapeño slices, finely chopped
- 1 tablespoon extra virgin olive oil

The spicy kick in the jalapeño dressing perfectly balances the sweetness of the mango. Mango doesn't brown after it has been cut, so you can chop ahead of time and store in the fridge.

Classics & New Classics

oodles &
oodles &
oodles &
oodles &
oodles &
Noodles &
Noodles

Zoodles
Zoodles
Zoodles
Zoodles
& Zoodles
& Zoodles
& Zoodl

# Hokkien noodle & snow pea salad

1   Toss the salad ingredients together. Season to taste then tip into your lunchbox.

2   Combine the dressing ingredients in a small jar or container with a tight-fitting lid.

3   Pour the dressing over the salad just before serving and toss well.

150 g (5½ oz) cooked thin hokkien (egg) noodles, rinsed and drained

100 g (3½ oz) snow peas (mangetout), halved

1 small orange, segmented

¼ avocado, sliced

Almond miso dressing
–   2 tablespoons orange juice
–   1½ tablespoons almond butter
–   1 tablespoon rice wine vinegar
–   2 teaspoons white miso paste
–   2 teaspoons toasted sesame seeds

Orange adds a zesty citrus note to this fresh noodle salad. This recipe also works well with soba or instant (ramen) noodles instead of the hokkien noodles.

Noodles & Zoodles

# Soba noodle, tofu & sugar snap pea salad

1 Toss the salad ingredients together. Season to taste then tip into your lunchbox.

2 Combine the dressing ingredients in a small jar or container with a tight-fitting lid.

3 Pour the dressing over the salad just before serving and toss well.

180 g (6½ oz) cooked, rinsed and drained soba noodles

100 g (3½ oz) sugar snap peas, blanched

50 g (1¾ oz) silken tofu, cubed

2 radishes, thinly sliced

Soy & wasabi dressing
– 1½ tablespoons soy sauce or tamari
– 1 tablespoon rice wine vinegar
– 2 teaspoons toasted sesame oil
– 1 teaspoon wasabi paste (or to taste)
– 1 teaspoon honey

In this Japanese-inspired noodle salad, the silken texture of the tofu plays against the crunch of the radish and sugar snap peas. The wasabi dressing adds a little sharpness.

Noodles & Zoodles

# Spicy ramen noodle & chicken salad

1   Toss the salad ingredients together. Season to taste then tip into your lunchbox.

2   Combine the dressing ingredients in a small jar or container with a tight-fitting lid.

3   Pour the dressing over the salad just before serving and toss well.

200 g (7 oz) instant (ramen) noodles, cooked, rinsed and drained

50 g (1¾ oz) sugar snap peas, sliced and blanched

100 g (3½ oz) shredded cooked chicken

2 handfuls of baby spinach leaves

Spicy peanut dressing
- 3 tablespoons peanut butter
- 1½ tablespoons rice wine vinegar
- 1 teaspoon toasted sesame oil
- 1 teaspoon sriracha sauce
- juice of ½ lime

The dressing in this recipe calls for sriracha —
a hot, spicy red sauce. If you prefer to avoid spice,
omit it or use another sauce instead.

Noodles & Zoodles

# Green tea noodles with salmon & crunchy greens

1 Toss the salad ingredients together. Season to taste then tip into your lunchbox.

2 Combine the dressing ingredients in a small jar or container with a tight-fitting lid.

3 Pour the dressing over the salad just before serving and toss well.

180 g (6½ oz) cooked, rinsed and drained green tea soba noodles

50 g (1¾ oz) green beans, sliced and blanched

85 g (3 oz) raw sashimi-grade salmon, sliced

½ short cucumber, thinly sliced

Sesame miso dressing
- 1 tablespoon white miso paste
- 1 tablespoon rice wine vinegar
- 1 tablespoon mirin
- 2 teaspoons toasted sesame seeds
- 1 teaspoon minced ginger

Green tea is a popular flavour in Japan, where it's added to a range of foods, including soba noodles. It pairs beautifully with the raw salmon, green beans and cucumber in this dish.

Noodles & Zoodles

# Antipasto noodle salad

1 Cook the pasta in a saucepan of boiling salted water for 2–3 minutes, until cooked, then drain and cool.

2 Toss the salad ingredients together. Season to taste then tip into your lunchbox.

3 Combine the dressing ingredients in a small jar or container with a tight-fitting lid.

4 Pour the dressing over the salad just before serving and toss well.

100 g (3½ oz) fresh fettuccine pasta

2 roasted red capsicums (bell peppers), sliced

2 marinated artichoke hearts, quartered

6 balls of cherry bocconcini cheese

Pesto dressing
- 2 tablespoons store-bought pesto
- 1 tablespoon red wine vinegar
- pinch of dried chilli flakes

This salad is so simple to put together – it just requires some shopping at your local Mediterranean or supermarket deli. If you prefer, make your own pesto ahead of time.

Noodles & Zoodles

# Herby zoodles with prawns

1. Toss the salad ingredients together. Season to taste then tip into your lunchbox.

2. Combine the dressing ingredients in a small jar or container with a tight-fitting lid.

3. Pour the dressing over the salad just before serving and toss well.

1 zucchini (courgette), spiralised

5–6 large cooked peeled prawns (shrimp)

100 g (3½ oz) drained tinned cannellini beans

handful of mint leaves

Preserved lemon dressing
- 2 tablespoons extra virgin olive oil
- 1½ tablespoons lemon juice
- ¼ preserved lemon, rind only, finely chopped
- pinch of dried chilli flakes

Mint and the preserved lemon dressing are a great combination with the prawns in this recipe. Zucchini can be bought already spiralised in the fresh vegetable section of most supermarkets.

Noodles & Zoodles

# Cucumber & green apple zoodles with salmon

1   Toss the salad ingredients together. Season to taste then tip into your lunchbox.

2   Combine the dressing ingredients in a small jar or container with a tight-fitting lid.

3   Pour the dressing over the salad just before serving and toss well.

80 g (2¾ oz) hot-smoked pepper salmon, flaked

1 short cucumber, spiralised into wide ribbons

½ baby fennel, thinly shaved, fronds reserved

1 small granny smith apple, cored and spiralised

Creamy lemon & herb dressing
- 3 tablespoons crème fraîche
- 2 teaspoons lemon juice
- 2 teaspoons finely chopped dill
- 2 teaspoons finely chopped mint leaves

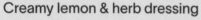

Hot-smoked salmon is often available in various styles in the supermarket. This recipe calls for pepper-crusted salmon, but you can also use a plain version.

Noodles & Zoodles

# Thai red curry chicken zoodles

1. Toss the salad ingredients together. Season to taste then tip into your lunchbox.

2. Combine the dressing ingredients in a small jar or container with a tight-fitting lid.

3. Pour the dressing over the salad just before serving and toss well.

100 g (3½ oz) shredded cooked chicken

1 carrot, spiralised

1 zucchini (courgette), spiralised

handful of mixed Asian herbs, such as Thai basil, Vietnamese mint and coriander (cilantro)

Thai red curry dressing
- 2 tablespoons coconut cream
- 1 teaspoon mirin
- 1 teaspoon store-bought Thai red curry paste
- juice and zest of ½ lime

Here's a simple salad version of a Thai chicken curry. If you prefer, opt for rice noodles instead of the spiralised vegetables.

Noodles & Zoodles

# Asparagus & zucchini zoodles

1 Toss the salad ingredients together. Season to taste then tip into your lunchbox.

2 Combine the dressing ingredients in a small jar or container with a tight-fitting lid.

3 Pour the dressing over the salad just before serving and toss well.

5–6 asparagus spears, thinly shaved

1 large zucchini (courgette), spiralised into wide ribbons

large handful of rocket (arugula)

30 g (1 oz) shaved pecorino

Green olive dressing
- 4–5 small pitted green olives, finely chopped
- 1 tablespoon lemon juice
- 2 teaspoons extra virgin olive oil
- 1 teaspoon finely chopped parsley

This salad is the perfect choice in spring, when asparagus is at its peak. If you come across it, white asparagus – or a combination of white and green asparagus – could be used here.

Noodles & Zoodles

# Chilli tuna & stuffed red capsicum pappardelle

1 Cook the pasta in a saucepan of boiling salted water for 2–3 minutes, until cooked, then drain and cool.

2 Toss the salad ingredients together. Season to taste then tip into your lunchbox.

3 Combine the dressing ingredients in a small jar or container with a tight-fitting lid.

4 Pour the dressing over the salad just before serving and toss well.

100 g (3½ oz) fresh pappardelle pasta

4 feta-stuffed baby red bell peppers (capsicums), halved (available from delis)

95 g (3¼ oz) tin tuna in chilli oil, undrained

handful of parsley

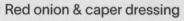

Red onion & caper dressing
- 2 tablespoons lemon juice
- 1½ tablespoons extra virgin olive oil
- 1½ tablespoons finely chopped red onion
- 1½ teaspoons baby capers

There are so many varieties of fresh pasta available in supermarkets, which cook in just a few minutes. They are the perfect choice for getting pasta salads organised in 5 minutes.

Noodles & Zoodles

# Pumpkin zoodle & prosciutto salad

1 Toss the salad ingredients together. Season to taste then tip into your lunchbox.

2 Combine the dressing ingredients in a small jar or container with a tight-fitting lid.

3 Pour the dressing over the salad just before serving and toss well.

200 g (7 oz) pumpkin (winter squash) zoodles, blanched, refreshed and cooled

3 prosciutto slices, torn

handful of chopped radicchio

40 g (1½ oz) blue cheese, crumbled

Balsamic dijon dressing
- 2 tablespoons extra virgin olive oil
- 1 tablespoon balsamic vinegar
- 1 teaspoon dijon mustard
- 1 teaspoon honey

If you have a good spiraliser, you can spiralise many different fruits and vegetables. Alternatively, seek out pre-spiralised vegetables for an even quicker salad.

Noodles & Zoodles

# Chicken & mango noodle salad

1. Toss the salad ingredients together. Season to taste then tip into your lunchbox.

2. Combine the dressing ingredients in a small jar or container with a tight-fitting lid.

3. Pour the dressing over the salad just before serving and toss well.

100 g (3½ oz) cooked, rinsed and drained vermicelli noodles

100 g (3½ oz) shredded cooked chicken

½ mango, sliced

handful of coriander (cilantro) leaves

Sweet chilli & lime dressing
- 2½ tablespoons sweet chilli sauce
- juice and zest of ½ lime
- 2 teaspoons finely chopped red onion
- 2 teaspoons finely chopped mint leaves
- 1 teaspoon minced ginger

A Southeast Asian-inspired noodle salad that uses sweet chilli sauce in the dressing, this salad is best enjoyed in summer, when mangoes are at their delicious peak.

Noodles & Zoodles

# Chicken, cabbage, pear & carrot zoodles

1 Toss the salad ingredients together. Season to taste then tip into your lunchbox.

2 Combine the dressing ingredients in a small jar or container with a tight-fitting lid.

3 Pour the dressing over the salad just before serving and toss well.

2 white or purple carrots, spiralised

100 g (3½ oz) shredded cooked chicken

1 nashi pear, spiralised

handful of finely shredded red cabbage

Ginger vinaigrette dressing
- 1½ tablespoons rice vinegar
- 1½ tablespoons mirin
  2 teaspoons toasted sesame oil
- 2 teaspoons toasted sesame seeds
- 1 teaspoon minced ginger

Carrots are not only orange! Good greengrocers will often stock purple and white carrot varieties, alongside the more common orange ones. Feel free to substitute whichever variety you like.

Noodles & Zoodles

# Japanese edamame & zoodle salad

1 Toss the salad ingredients together. Season to taste then tip into your lunchbox.

2 Combine the dressing ingredients in a small jar or container with a tight-fitting lid.

3 Pour the dressing over the salad just before serving and toss well.

200 g (7 oz) spiralised zucchini (courgette)

1 short cucumber, shredded

100 g (3½ oz) cooked edamame beans

3 spring (green) onions, thinly sliced

1 tablespoon black sesame seeds

Sesame & ginger dressing
– ½ teaspoon sesame oil
– 1 tablespoon rice wine vinegar
– 1 tablespoon soy sauce or tamari
– 1 teaspoon minced ginger

A fantastic alternative to a classic soba noodle salad, zoodles are the perfect vehicle for light and fresh Japanese flavours. To save a bit of time, buy frozen shelled edamame.

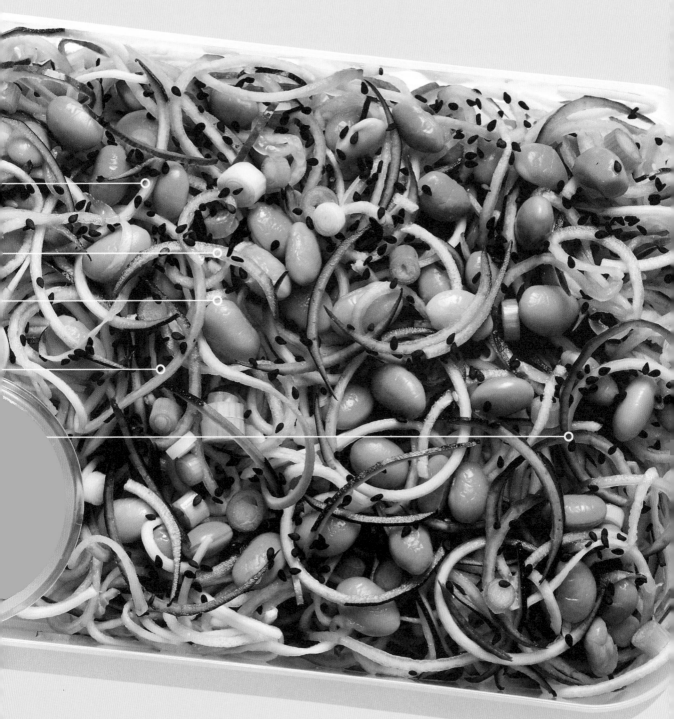

Noodles & Zoodles

# Vietnamese noodle salad

1. Place the peanuts in a small, airtight container.

2. Toss the remaining salad ingredients together. Season to taste then tip into your lunchbox.

3. Combine the dressing ingredients in a small jar or container with a tight-fitting lid.

4. Pour the dressing and scatter the peanuts over the salad just before serving and toss well.

1 tablespoon salted peanuts

80 g (2¾ oz) cooked and cooled vermicelli noodles

large handful of shredded carrot

1 spring (green) onion, sliced

50 g (1¾ oz) snow peas (mangetout), sliced

1 short cucumber, diced

handful each of coriander (cilantro) and mint leaves

Nuoc cham dressing
- 1 tablespoon fish sauce
- 1½ tablespoons lime juice
- 2 teaspoons rice wine vinegar
- 1 teaspoon caster (superfine) sugar
- ½ red bird's eye chilli, deseeded and sliced
- ½ teaspoon minced garlic

This recipe uses fish sauce, but you can easily substite vegan fish sauce. There are many different versions available, generally made from ingredients, such as mushroom, soy and seaweed.

Noodles & Zoodles

# Rainbow noodle salad

1   Toss the salad ingredients together. Season to taste then tip into your lunchbox.

2   Combine the dressing ingredients in a small jar or container with a tight-fitting lid.

3   Pour the dressing over the salad just before serving and toss well.

1 small zucchini (courgette), spiralised

1 small golden beetroot (beet), spiralised

¼ orange bell pepper (capsicum), sliced

1 small carrot, spiralised

handful of shredded red cabbage

handful of grape (baby plum) tomatoes, halved

Orange–miso dressing
- 2 tablespoons orange juice
- 2 teaspoons white miso paste
- 1 teaspoon sesame oil
- freshly ground black pepper, to taste

This colourful salad is a fantastic way to eat more veggies. You can mix it up based on what's in season – try red beetroot (beet), white cabbage, and yellow, green or red bell pepper (capsicum).

Noodles & Zoodles

# Chicken soba noodle salad

1. Toss the soba noodles with a little sesame oil. Add the remaining salad ingredients and toss together. Season to taste then tip into your lunchbox.

2. Combine the dressing ingredients in a small jar or container with a tight-fitting lid.

3. Pour the dressing over the salad just before serving and toss well.

180 g (6½ oz) cooked soba noodles, cooled under running water, drained

sesame oil, for drizzling

100 g (3½ oz) shredded cooked chicken

1 spring (green) onion, thinly sliced

50 g (1¾ oz) snow peas (mangetout), sliced

handful of shredded carrot

Sesame dressing
- 1 tablespoon toasted sesame seeds
- 1 tablespoon rice wine vinegar
- 1 tablespoon light soy sauce
- ¾ teaspoon caster (superfine) sugar
- 2 teaspoons sesame oil

The sesame dressing is a lighter take on Japanese goma, usually made with mayonnaise. You can, of course, add some kewpie mayo – just thin it out with water and add a little less sugar.

Noodles & Zoodles

# Chilli & lime tuna noodle salad

1 Toss the salad ingredients together, except the lime wedges, then tip into your lunchbox.

2 Squeeze the lime wedges over the salad just before serving and toss well.

95 g (3¼ oz) tin tuna in chilli oil, undrained

150 g (5½ oz) instant (ramen) noodles, cooked, cooled under running water, drained

large handful of baby spinach leaves

1 celery stalk, sliced

freshly ground black pepper, to taste

lime wedges

This fresh and summery salad uses the chilli oil from the tuna tin as the dressing. If you would prefer less chilli, you can drain the tuna and use a little extra virgin olive oil instead.

Noodles & Zoodles

# Zoodle pesto salad

1 Massage the lemon juice and salt into the zoodles, then gently stir in the remaining ingredients. Tip into your lunchbox.

2 Place the pesto in a small, airtight container.

3 Stir the pesto through the salad just before serving and toss well.

juice of 1 lemon

pinch of salt

250 g (9 oz) spiralised zucchini (courgette)

handful of grape (baby plum) tomatoes, halved

freshly ground black pepper, to taste

small handful of basil leaves, larger leaves roughly chopped

2 tablespoons pesto

This dish is like a classic Italian pasta in salad form. There's no need to pre-cook the zoodles, as they marinate in the lemon juice and salt.

Noodles & Zoodles

# Broccolini & sesame soba noodle salad

1  Blanch the broccolini in boiling salted water for 2 minutes. Drain and refresh under cold running water.

2  Toss the broccolini with the remaining salad ingredients, then tip into your lunchbox.

3  Combine the dressing ingredients in a small jar or container with a tight-fitting lid.

4  Pour the dressing over the salad just before serving and toss well.

1 bunch broccolini, cut into 5 cm (2 in) lengths

180 g (6½ oz) cooked soba noodles, cooled under running water, drained

2 spring (green) onions, thinly sliced

2 tablespoons toasted sesame seeds

Honey sesame dressing
- 1 teaspoon minced ginger
- 2 teaspoons sesame oil
- 1 teaspoon honey
- 1 tablespoon rice wine vinegar
- 1½ tablespoons light soy sauce
- freshly ground white pepper, to taste

Simple to make, yet packed with flavour,
this salad is best when broccolini is in season.
If it's unavailable, just use broccoli instead.

Noodles & Zoodles

# Satay chopped salad

1. Place the crispy-fried noodles in an airtight container.

2. Toss the remaining salad ingredients together, season to taste, then tip into your lunchbox.

3. Combine the dressing ingredients in a small jar or container with a tight-fitting lid.

4. Mix the crispy-fried noodles into the salad just before serving, pour over the dressing and toss well.

30 g (1 oz) crispy-fried noodles

2 spring (green) onions, sliced

handful of shredded red cabbage

handful of shredded carrot

1 red bird's eye chilli, finely chopped

2 radishes, thinly sliced

handful each of dill, mint and coriander (cilantro), chopped

Satay dressing
- ½ teaspoon minced garlic
- ½ teaspoon minced ginger
- 2 tablespoons peanut butter
- 2 teaspoons hoisin sauce
- juice of 1 lime
- 1 teaspoon grated palm sugar
- 1 tablespoon fish sauce

The satay dressing packs a flavour punch in this crunchy, summery salad. If you have dietary restrictions, crispy-fried noodles are now available in gluten-free options.

Noodles & Zoodles

# Crunchy ramen noodle salad

1. Toss the salad ingredients together, then tip into your lunchbox.

2. Combine the dressing ingredients in a small jar or container with a tight-fitting lid.

3. Pour the dressing over the salad just before serving and toss well.

1 spring (green) onion, thinly sliced

80 g (2¾ oz) shredded wombok (Chinese cabbage)

85 g (3 oz) instant (ramen) noodles, broken into pieces

handful of shredded carrot

1 tablespoon black sesame seeds

30 g (¼ cup) slivered almonds

Sesame soy dressing
- 1 tablespoon light soy sauce
- 1 teaspoon sesame oil
- 1 teaspoon black vinegar
- 1 tablespoon neutral-flavoured oil
- ½ teaspoon sugar
- ½ teaspoon minced ginger

Adding the noodles to the salad in the morning gives them a chance to soften. If you want your salad super crunchy, leave the noodles in the packet and toss them through just before you eat.

Noodles & Zoodles

# Sesame & avocado soba noodle salad

1  Toss the soba noodles with a little of the sesame oil.

2  Squeeze the lemon juice over the avocado pieces and gently toss to coat.

3  Toss the soba noodles and avocado with the remaining salad ingredients, then tip into your lunchbox.

4  Combine the dressing ingredients in a small jar or container with a tight-fitting lid.

5  Pour the dressing over the salad just before serving and toss well.

180 g (6½ oz) cooked soba noodles, cooled under running water, drained

sesame oil, for drizzling

juice of ½ lemon

½ avocado, chopped

50 g (1¾ oz) snow peas (mangetout), trimmed and sliced diagonally

2 spring (green) onions, sliced diagonally

1 tablespoon black sesame seeds

### Soy sesame dressing
- 2 tablespoons soy sauce or tamari
- 1 tablespoon rice wine vinegar
- 1 tablespoon mirin
- 1 teaspoon sesame oil

'Soba' is the Japanese word for buckwheat – a gluten-free grain popular throughout Asia. If you are avoiding gluten, check the ingredients, as some noodles sold as soba are not gluten free.

Noodles & Zoodles

# Sort-of dan dan noodles

1  Toss the shirataki noodles with a little sesame oil. Add the remaining salad ingredients and toss together, then tip into your lunchbox.

2  Combine the dressing ingredients in a small jar or container with a tight-fitting lid.

3  Pour the dressing over the salad just before serving and toss well.

200 g (7 oz) cooked shirataki (konjac) noodles

1 teaspoon sesame oil

handful of roughly chopped coriander (cilantro) leaves

½ short cucumber, sliced

1 long red chilli, deseeded and thinly sliced

2 tablespoons chopped pickled mustard greens

2 tablespoons roasted peanuts, chopped

Tahini chilli dressing
–  1½ tablespoons tahini
–  1 tablespoon chinkiang or black vinegar
–  3 teaspoons vegan chilli oil
–  2 teaspoons light soy sauce
–  ½ teaspoon minced garlic
–  pinch of caster (superfine) sugar

This vegan take of the popular Sichuan dish calls for shirataki noodles, ultra-low-calorie noodles made from konjac – an Asian root vegetable. You can replace them with whatever noodles you prefer.

Noodles & Zoodles

# Orange, carrot & beet zoodle salad

1. Zest half the orange, then cut in half. Juice the zested half, then place the juice, zest and remaining dressing ingredients in a small jar or container with a tight-fitting lid. Season the dressing to taste.

2. Peel the other half of the orange and cut into bite-sized pieces. Toss the orange pieces with the remaining salad ingredients, then tip into your lunchbox.

3. Pour the dressing over the salad and toss just before serving.

1 orange

2–3 medjool dates, thinly sliced

1 beetroot (beet), spiralised

small handful of roughly chopped pistachios

small handful of chopped parsley

1 carrot, spiralised

Orange & cinnamon dressing
- 2 tablespoons extra virgin olive oil
- pinch of ground cinnamon

An explosion of colour and flavour, this salad is a breeze to throw together. If you want to make this even quicker, grab some pre-spiralised vegetables from the supermarket.

Noodles & Zoodles

# Crispy soy noodles

1 Place the crispy-fried noodles in an airtight container.

2 Toss the remaining salad ingredients together, then tip into your lunchbox.

3 Combine the dressing ingredients in a small jar or container with a tight-fitting lid.

4 Mix the crispy-fried noodles into the salad just before serving, pour over the dressing and toss well.

60 g (2 oz) crispy-fried noodles

handful of shredded carrot

handful of shredded wombok (Chinese cabbage)

1 tablespoon finely chopped chives

3–4 radishes, very thinly sliced

Sesame soy dressing
- 1 tablespoon light soy sauce
- 1 tablespoon neutral-flavoured oil
- 1 teaspoon sesame oil
- 1 teaspoon chinkiang or black vinegar
- ½ teaspoon caster (superfine) sugar
- ½ teaspoon minced ginger

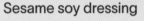

This salad combines the crunch of crisp noodles with colourful and tasty vegetables alongside an Asian-style sesame dressing.

Noodles & Zoodles

# Mushroom & pesto zoodles

1 Heat a splash of oil in a small frying pan and fry the mushrooms and garlic for 2–3 minutes. Remove to cool.

2 Toss the mushroom and remaining salad ingredients together, then tip into your lunchbox.

3 Combine the dressing ingredients in a small jar or container with a tight-fitting lid. Season to taste.

4 Pour the dressing over the salad just before serving and toss well.

olive oil, for pan-frying

4–5 button mushrooms, thinly sliced

1 teaspoon minced garlic

1 zucchini (courgette), spiralised

4–5 cherry tomatoes, halved

2 tablespoons toasted pine nuts

4–5 pitted kalamata olives, halved

Cashew pesto dressing
- 2 tablespoons vegan pesto
- 2 tablespoons cashew cream
- squeeze of lemon juice

This salad is a nod to the Mediterranean. The dressing calls for both cashew cream and vegan pesto – both of which can be found in health food stores and in some supermarkets.

Noodles & Zoodles

# Vietnamese salad with pickled veg

1  Dissolve the sugar in the boiling water. Add the vinegar. Place the carrot and cucumber in a small container with a tight-fitting lid. Pour the brine over, pop the lid on and give it a good shake.

2  Combine the dressing ingredients in a small jar or container with a tight-fitting lid.

3  Toss the remaining ingredients together, then tip into your lunchbox.

4  Just before serving, drain the pickled veg and add them to the salad, then pour over the dressing and toss well.

3 tablespoons caster (superfine) sugar

3 tablespoons boiling water

3 tablespoons white vinegar

small handful each of shredded carrot and cucumber

150 g (5½ oz) cooked vermicelli noodles

small handful each of coriander (cilantro) and mint leaves

1 spring (green) onion, sliced

Nuoc cham dressing
-  1 tablespoon vegan fish sauce
-  1½ tablespoons lime juice
-  2 teaspoons rice wine vinegar
-  1 teaspoon caster (superfine) sugar
-  ½ red bird's eye chilli, deseeded and sliced
-  ½ teaspoon minced garlic

Although this recipe looks complicated, it's really just a few elements thrown together. If you want to save a little more time, use store-bought pickled vegetables and nuoc cham dressing.

Noodles & Zoodles

# Ramen noodle salad

1  Toss the salad ingredients together, then tip into your lunchbox.

2  Combine the dressing ingredients in a small jar or container with a tight-fitting lid.

3  Pour the dressing over the salad just before serving and toss well.

100 g (3½ oz) instant (ramen) noodles, cooked, cooled under running water, drained

½ carrot, spiralised

50 g (1¾ oz) snow peas (mangetout), thinly sliced

handful of bean sprouts

handful of mint leaves

2 spring (green) onions, thinly sliced

Lemon soy dressing
–  1 tablespoon light soy sauce
–  1 tablespoon lemon juice
–  2 teaspoons maple syrup
–  1 teaspoon minced ginger
–  1 teaspoon minced garlic

Instant (ramen) noodles are available in many guises – in different widths and lengths, some gluten-free and made with rice – so feel free to explore your options.

Noodles & Zoodles

# Ranch zoodles

1 Toss the salad ingredients together, then tip into your lunchbox.

2 Combine the dressing ingredients in a small jar or container with a tight-fitting lid. Season to taste.

3 Pour the dressing over the salad just before serving and toss well.

1 celery stalk, thinly sliced

1 zucchini (courgette), spiralised

¼ red onion, thinly sliced

3–4 radishes, thinly sliced

50 g (1¾ oz) vegan feta, crumbled

small handful of pitted kalamata olives, sliced

small handful of chopped toasted pecans

Ranch dressing
- 60 g (¼ cup) vegan mayonnaise
- 2 tablespoons soy milk
- ½ teaspoon dried parsley
- ½ teaspoon dried chives
- ½ teaspoon garlic powder
- ½ teaspoon onion powder

Ranch is a typically American salad dressing made with buttermilk. We've made this classic vegan by using plant-based dairy. This is a versatile dressing you can use on many different salads.

Noodles & Zoodles

# Crunchy peanut noodles

1. Toss the salad ingredients together, then tip into your lunchbox.

2. Combine the dressing ingredients with 2 teaspoons of water in a small jar or container with a tight-fitting lid.

3. Pour the dressing over the salad just before serving and toss well.

85 g (3 oz) instant (ramen) noodles, broken into pieces

small handful of shredded red cabbage

¼ red bell pepper (capsicum), thinly sliced

1 spring (green) onion, sliced

2 tablespoons crushed peanuts

small handful each of coriander (cilantro) and basil leaves

Spicy peanut sauce
- 2 tablespoons crunchy peanut butter
- 1 tablespoon light soy sauce
- 1 tablespoon lime juice
- 2 teaspoons maple syrup
- 1 small red bird's eye chilli, deseeded and diced

If you prefer, keep the noodles separate from your salad ingredients and mix them in at the last moment – this will keep them nice and crunchy.

Noodles & Zoodles

# Spicy papaya noodle salad

1 For the dressing, pound the chillies and garlic using a mortar and pestle. Add the peanuts and miso paste and pound until you have a rough paste. Stir in the palm sugar, vegan fish sauce and lime juice. Transfer to a small container with a tight-fitting lid.

2 Toss the salad ingredients together, then tip into your lunchbox.

3 Pour the dressing over the salad just before serving and toss well. Serve with lime wedges.

100 g (3½ oz) cooked vermicelli noodles, cooled under running water, drained

¼ small papaya, shredded

handful of cherry tomatoes, halved

handful of green beans, chopped into 2 cm (¾ in) lengths

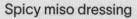

Spicy miso dressing
- 2 red bird's eye chillies
- 2 garlic cloves
- 1½ tablespoons roasted unsalted peanuts
- 1 tablespoon red miso paste
- 1 tablespoon grated palm sugar
- 2 tablespoons vegan fish sauce
- juice of 1 lime, plus extra wedges to serve

This recipe is a nod to the popular, spicy Thai salad som tam. We've replaced green papaya with ripe papaya and snake (yard-long) beans with green beans, as well as adding in noodles.

Noodles & Zoodles

# Italian noodle salad

1  Cook the pasta in a saucepan of boiling salted water for 2–3 minutes, until cooked, then drain. Stir the pesto through the pasta and cool.

2  Toss the pasta with the remaining salad ingredients, season to taste, then tip into your lunchbox.

150 g (5½ oz) fresh vegan fettuccine, spaghetti or other wheat noodles

2 tablespoons homemade or store-bought vegan pesto

handful of grape (baby plum) tomatoes, halved

small handful of basil leaves

1 roasted red capsicum (bell pepper), sliced

To keep this simple salad vegan, make sure you choose pasta that is egg-free, and that the pesto is made without parmesan.

Noodles & Zoodles

Grains &
Grains &
Grains &
Grains &
Grains

Seeds
Seeds
Seeds
& Seeds
& Seed

# Edamame & brown rice salad

1  Blanch the broccolini and edamame beans in boiling salted water for 2 minutes. Drain and refresh in cold water, then slice the broccolini into 3 cm (1¼ inch) pieces.

2  Toss with the remaining salad ingredients, season to taste, then tip into your lunchbox.

3  Combine the dressing ingredients in a small jar or container with a tight-fitting lid.

4  Pour the dressing over the salad just before serving and toss well.

3 broccolini stems

80 g (½ cup) frozen edamame beans

150 g (1 cup) cooked and cooled brown rice

½ avocado, sliced

Sesame miso dressing
–  1 tablespoon white miso paste
–  1 tablespoon rice wine vinegar
–  1 tablespoon mirin
–  2 teaspoons toasted sesame seeds
–  1 teaspoon minced ginger

Edamame beans – or soy beans – are available in the freezer section of some supermarkets and in Asian grocers. They make a great snack on their own, sprinkled with some sea salt.

Grains & Seeds

# Chicken & rice salad with ginger soy dressing

1. Toss the salad ingredients together and season to taste, then tip into your lunchbox.

2. Combine the dressing ingredients in a small jar or container with a tight-fitting lid.

3. Pour the dressing over the salad just before serving and toss well.

50 g (1¾ oz) snow peas (mangetout), sliced

100 g (3½ oz) shredded cooked chicken

150 g (1 cup) cooked and cooled rice

large handful of mixed micro herbs

Ginger soy dressing
- 1½ tablespoons macadamia or other neutral-flavoured oil
- 1 tablespoon rice wine vinegar
- 1 tablespoon tamari or soy sauce
- 2 teaspoons minced ginger
- 1 teaspoon toasted sesame oil

If you prefer a nuttier flavour — and a little more fibre — in your salad, opt for brown rice here. Micro herbs can be found in most good-quality greengrocers.

Grains & Seeds

# Salmon poke bowl with black rice

1. Toss the salad ingredients together and season to taste, then tip into your lunchbox.

2. Combine the dressing ingredients in a small jar or container with a tight-fitting lid.

3. Pour the dressing over the salad just before serving and toss well.

100 g (3½ oz) raw sashimi-grade salmon, diced

150 g (1 cup) cooked and cooled black rice

½ avocado, diced

75 g (½ cup) podded cooked edamame beans

Sweet chilli soy dressing
- 1½ tablespoons soy sauce or tamari
- 1½ tablespoons sweet chilli sauce
- 2 teaspoons rice wine vinegar
- 1 teaspoon toasted sesame oil
- 1 spring (green) onion, thinly sliced

Poke bowls originated in Hawaii, but are now loved around the world. They typically contain raw fish, rice and salad, and make a quick, nutritious lunch.

Grains & Seeds

# Persian couscous salad

1 Toss the salad ingredients together and season to taste, then tip into your lunchbox.

2 Combine the dressing ingredients in a small jar or container with a tight-fitting lid.

3 Pour the dressing over the salad just before serving and toss well.

150 g (1 cup) cooked and cooled couscous

100 g (3½ oz) shredded cooked chicken

70 g (2½ oz) diced mixed dried fruits (apricot, cherries, figs)

2 tablespoons chopped pistachios

Lemon & sumac dressing
- 2 tablespoons extra virgin olive oil
- juice and zest of ½ lemon
- 1 tablespoon finely diced shallot
- 2 teaspoons chopped mint leaves
- ½ teaspoon ground sumac

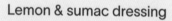

Moreish dried fruits and nutty pistachios combined with couscous and shredded chicken – what a delight! This hearty couscous-based salad is a feast for the senses.

Grains & Seeds

# Red quinoa autumn salad

1  Toss the salad ingredients together and season to taste, then tip into your lunchbox.

2  Combine the dressing ingredients in a small jar or container with a tight-fitting lid.

3  Pour the dressing over the salad just before serving and toss well.

150 g (1 cup) cooked and cooled red quinoa

handful of chopped red kale leaves

100 g (3½ oz) smoked chicken breast, sliced

2 tablespoons toasted walnuts, chopped

Sherry vinegar & shallot dressing
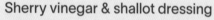
–  2 tablespoons extra virgin olive oil
–  1½ tablespoons Spanish sherry vinegar
–  1 tablespoon finely diced shallot
–  2 teaspoons honey

You can replace the red kale in this salad with green, or whatever salad leaves you have at hand. Kale can be tough, so tenderise the leaves ahead of time by massaging with a little lemon juice.

Grains & Seeds

# Couscous, tomato, cucumber & feta salad

1  Toss the salad ingredients together and season to taste, then tip into your lunchbox.

2  Combine the dressing ingredients in a small jar or container with a tight-fitting lid.

3  Pour the dressing over the salad just before serving and toss well.

1 short cucumber, sliced

handful of cherry tomatoes, halved

150 g (1 cup) cooked and cooled couscous

40 g (1½ oz) feta cheese, crumbled

Creamy dill dressing
- 3 tablespoons Greek yoghurt
- juice and zest of ½ lemon
- 2 teaspoons finely chopped dill
- ½ teaspoon minced garlic

Juicy tomatoes, salty, creamy feta and crisp, crunchy cucumber evoke memories of the Mediterranean in this simple salad. A creamy, tangy dill dressing plays a perfect complement.

Grains & Seeds

# Black quinoa & roasted pumpkin salad

1 Toss the salad ingredients together and season to taste, then tip into your lunchbox.

2 Combine the dressing ingredients in a small jar or container with a tight-fitting lid.

3 Pour the dressing over the salad just before serving and toss well.

150 g (1 cup) cooked and cooled black quinoa

200 g (7 oz) left-over roasted pumpkin (winter squash), diced

2 tablespoons honey-spiced almonds or pecans, some chopped

large handful of chopped kale

Sherry vinegar & mustard dressing
- 2 tablespoons extra virgin olive oil
- 1½ tablespoons Spanish sherry vinegar
- 1 teaspoon honey
- 1 teaspoon wholegrain mustard

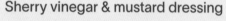

This recipe calls for left-over pumpkin, but you can use whatever left-over roast vegetables you may have, including sweet potato, carrot, zucchini or potato.

Grains & Seeds

# Bulgur & roasted veg salad

1. Toss the salad ingredients together and season to taste, then tip into your lunchbox.

2. Combine the dressing ingredients in a small jar or container with a tight-fitting lid.

3. Pour the dressing over the salad just before serving and toss well.

150 g (1 cup) cooked and cooled bulgur

200 g (7 oz) left-over roasted baby vegetables

100 g (3½ oz) drained tinned chickpeas

handful of mint leaves

Harissa yoghurt dressing
- 3 tablespoons Greek yoghurt
- 2 teaspoons lemon juice
- 1 teaspoon harissa paste
- 1 teaspoon pomegranate molasses

The harissa in the dressing really gives this tasty salad a little spark. Feel free to increase the amount used if you like a little more heat.

# Chicken, mint & couscous salad

1 Toss the salad ingredients together and season to taste, then tip into your lunchbox.

2 Combine the dressing ingredients in a small jar or container with a tight-fitting lid.

3 Pour the dressing over the salad just before serving and toss well.

100 g (3½ oz) shredded cooked chicken

150 g (1 cup) cooked and cooled couscous

large handful of roughly torn mint leaves

3 tablespoons currants

Lemon dressing
- 2 tablespoons extra virgin olive oil
- juice of ½ lemon

If you wanted to add a few more ingredients to this salad, you could always throw in a few different types of herbs. Parsley, basil and coriander would all be good additions.

Grains & Seeds

# California superfood salad

1  Toss the salad ingredients together, then tip into your lunchbox.

2  Combine the dressing ingredients in a small jar or container with a tight-fitting lid. Season to taste.

3  Pour the dressing over the salad just before serving and toss well.

75 g (2¾ oz) cooked quinoa

75 g (2¾ oz) drained tinned black beans

75 g (2¾ oz) drained tinned sweet corn kernels

handful of mixed grape (baby plum) tomatoes, halved

2 tablespoons grated parmesan

1 tablespoon puffed wild rice

handful of baby kale

1 tablespoon goji berries

Lime & jalapeño dressing
– 3 pickled jalapeño slices, finely chopped
– 2 tablespoons lime juice
– 1 tablespoon extra virgin olive oil
– ¼ teaspoon minced garlic

Puffed wild rice brings a fantastic crunch to this salad. It can be purchased from health food stores or other specialty retailers.

# Chicken & quinoa salad with salsa verde dressing

1  Toss the salad ingredients together, then tip into your lunchbox.

2  Combine the dressing ingredients in a small jar or container with a tight-fitting lid.

3  Pour the dressing over the salad just before serving and toss well.

100 g (3½ oz) shredded cooked chicken

150 g (1 cup) cooked quinoa

30 g (1 oz) toasted pine nuts

1 celery stalk, sliced

¼ green chilli, thinly sliced

2 radishes, quartered

1 spring (green) onion, sliced

Salsa verde dressing
-  small handful each of basil, mint and parsley, very finely chopped
-  ½ teaspoon minced garlic
-  1 tablespoon white wine vinegar
-  2 tablespoons extra virgin olive oil

A riot of green with so many fresh herbs.
The salsa verde dressing is an excellent sauce –
try it with steak or drizzled over roast vegetables.

Grains & Seeds

# Mediterranean couscous salad

1 Toss the salad ingredients together, then tip into your lunchbox.

2 Combine the dressing ingredients in a small jar or container with a tight-fitting lid. Season to taste.

3 Pour the dressing over the salad just before serving and toss well.

150 g (1 cup) cooked couscous

¼ red bell pepper (capsicum), diced

½ small short cucumber, diced

handful of grape (baby plum) tomatoes, halved

large handful of pitted kalamata olives

small handful of capers, rinsed and drained

small handful of parsley, roughly chopped

Preserved lemon dressing
- ¼ preserved lemon, rind only, finely chopped
- juice of ½ lemon
- 1 teaspoon honey
- 1½ teaspoons dijon mustard
- 2 tablespoons extra virgin olive oil

Preserved lemon brings a real brightness to this salad. If you have a little more time, try making this salad with moghrabieh – a larger variety of couscous, also known as pearl couscous.

Grains & Seeds

# Hot-smoked trout, watercress & quinoa salad

1. Toss the salad ingredients together, then tip into your lunchbox.

2. Combine the dressing ingredients in a small jar or container with a tight-fitting lid. Season to taste.

3. Pour the dressing over the salad and toss well just before serving.

75 g (2¾ oz) flaked hot-smoked trout

150 g (1 cup) cooked and cooled quinoa

large handful of watercress, tough stalks removed

½ small short cucumber, diced

juice of ½ lemon

Creamy horseradish dressing

- 2 teaspoons prepared horseradish
- juice of 1 lemon
- 2 teaspoons baby capers, chopped
- 1 tablespoon crème fraîche or yoghurt
- 1 tablespoon extra virgin olive oil

154

The peppery heat of the horseradish brings a wonderfully sophisticated bite to this salad. If you can't find hot-smoked trout, salmon will do just as well.

# Brown rice & herb salad

1 Toss the salad ingredients together, then tip into your lunchbox.

2 Combine the dressing ingredients in a small jar or container with a tight-fitting lid. Season to taste.

3 Pour the dressing over the salad just before serving and toss well.

150 g (1 cup) cooked and cooled brown rice

handful each of dill, parsley, coriander (cilantro) and mint, roughly chopped

2 spring (green) onions, sliced

40 g (¼ cup) raw almonds, roughly chopped

3 tablespoons currants

1 tablespoon each sunflower kernels and pumpkin seeds

Lemon & vinegar dressing
- juice of ½ lemon
- 1 tablespoon apple cider vinegar
- 2 tablespoons extra virgin olive oil

This salad is a great way to use up left-over rice. Otherwise, you can pre-cook some rice the night before, or use microwavable rice – just make sure it is cold before mixing in the other ingredients.

Grains & Seeds

# Chicken & peach bulgur salad

1  Place the bulgur in a jar or heatproof container with a tight-fitting lid. Pour in the stock or water and cover with the lid.

2  Place the pecans in a small, airtight container.

3  Toss the peach in the lime juice. Add the remaining salad ingredients and toss together, then tip into your lunchbox.

4  Combine the dressing ingredients in a small jar or container with a tight-fitting lid. Season to taste.

5  Before serving, fluff the bulgur with a fork and add to the salad along with the pecans and the dressing. Toss well.

45 g (¼ cup) bulgur

60 ml (¼ cup) just-boiled chicken stock or water

30 g (1 oz) toasted pecans, chopped

1 ripe peach, sliced

1 teaspoon lime juice

100 g (3½ oz) shredded cooked chicken

30 g (1 oz) feta, crumbled

small handful of basil leaves

Maple dressing
- 1½ teaspoons maple syrup
- 1 tablespoon apple cider vinegar
- 1 teaspoon dijon mustard
- 2 tablespoons extra virgin olive oil

If you have a little more time in the morning (and you'd rather not take an extra jar with you to work), cover the bulgur with just-boiled water and allow to stand for 10–15 minutes before adding to the salad.

Grains & Seeds

# Chicken couscous salad with feta & pomegranate

1 Toss the salad ingredients together, then tip into your lunchbox.

2 Combine the dressing ingredients in a small jar or container with a tight-fitting lid. Season to taste.

3 Pour the dressing over the salad just before serving and toss well.

150 g (1 cup) cooked and cooled couscous

100 g (3½ oz) shredded cooked chicken

handful of frozen pomegranate seeds

30 g (¼ cup) slivered almonds

30 g (1 oz) feta, crumbled

small handful each of mint leaves and parsley, chopped

Pomegranate dressing
- 1 tablespoon red wine vinegar
- 1 teaspoon pomegranate molasses
- 2 tablespoons extra virgin olive oil

This recipe calls for frozen pomegranate seeds
for the sake of convenience, but you can definitely
use fresh seeds if you have them.

161

Grains & Seeds

# Quinoa, grapefruit & golden beetroot salad

1. Place the goat's cheese in a small, airtight container.

2. Segment the grapefruit over a small bowl to catch the juice.

3. Whisk together the grapefruit juice and dressing ingredients. Season to taste and pour into a small jar or container with a tight-fitting lid.

4. Toss the grapefruit segments and remaining salad ingredients together, then tip into your lunchbox.

5. Pour the dressing over the salad and toss well. Dot the goat's cheese over the top.

30 g (1 oz) goat's cheese

1 small pink grapefruit

150 g (1 cup) cooked and cooled quinoa

100 g (5½ oz) cooked golden beetroot (beet), chopped into chunks

large handful of rocket (arugula)

¼ red onion, thinly sliced

Maple dressing
- 2 teaspoons maple syrup
- 2 teaspoons white wine vinegar
- 2 tablespoons extra virgin olive oil

Pre-cooked beetroot (beet) is available at good supermarkets. Golden beetroot brings a lovely colour and sweetness to this salad, but the more common red variety works just as well.

Grains & Seeds

# Turkish-style bulgur salad

1 Combine the bulgur, tomato paste and onion in a jar or heatproof container with a tight-fitting lid. Pour in the stock or water and cover with the lid.

2 Place the remaining salad ingredients in your lunchbox.

3 Combine the dressing ingredients in a small jar or container with a tight-fitting lid. Season to taste.

4 Before serving, fluff the bulgur with a fork and add to the salad along with the dressing. Toss well to combine.

90 g (½ cup) bulgur

2 teaspoons tomato paste (concentrated purée)

½ onion, finely chopped

125 ml (½ cup) just-boiled chicken stock or water

1 spring (green) onion, sliced

handful of grape (baby plum) tomatoes, halved

handful each of parsley and mint leaves, roughly chopped

Pomegranate dressing
- 1 teaspoon pomegranate molasses
- juice of ½ lemon
- 2 tablespoons extra virgin olive oil

This recipe is inspired by Turkish *kisir*, a mildly spiced bulgur salad sweetened with pomegranate molasses. If you prefer a more savoury flavour, use lemon juice instead of the molasses.

Grains & Seeds

# Brown rice, cranberry & rosemary salad

1 Squeeze the lemon juice over the apple and toss to combine. Toss through the remaining salad ingredients, then tip into your lunchbox.

2 Combine the dressing ingredients in a small jar or container with a tight-fitting lid. Season to taste.

3 Pour the dressing over the salad just before serving and toss well.

juice of ½ lemon

½ apple, thinly sliced

150 g (1 cup) cooked and cooled brown rice

1 teaspoon finely chopped rosemary leaves

1 tablespoon dried cranberries

2 tablespoons chopped roasted almonds

handful of rocket (arugula)

Maple dressing
- 2 teaspoons maple syrup
- 1 tablespoon apple cider vinegar
- 1 tablespoon extra virgin olive oil

166

This is a very hearty salad that's perfect for colder weather. The combination of textures here is fantastic, with the toothsome rice, chewy cranberries and crunchy roasted almonds.

Grains & Seeds

# Moroccan-spiced couscous salad

1 Heat 1 teaspoon of the olive oil in a small saucepan over medium heat, add the couscous and stir for 30 seconds. Stir in the tomato paste and ras el hanout, and pour the boiling water over. Remove from the heat, cover and set aside to cool.

2 Toss the couscous and remaining salad ingredients together, season to taste, then tip into your lunchbox.

2 teaspoons olive oil

60 g (⅓ cup) instant couscous

1 teaspoon tomato paste (concentrated purée)

1 teaspoon ras el hanout

185 ml (¾ cup) boiling water

3 artichokes in olive oil, roughly chopped

2 teaspoons finely chopped preserved lemon rind

½ red onion, finely chopped

handful of chopped parsley

juice of 1 lemon, plus lemon wedges to serve

Ras el hanout is a fragrant North African spice blend. It is a mix of up to 30 different spices. Thankfully, it can commonly be found – already mixed – in most supermarkets.

# Super seed salad

1  Toast the seeds in a dry frying pan over medium heat for about 3 minutes, until lightly toasted. Immediately transfer to a bowl to cool.

2  Meanwhile, massage the lemon juice into the baby kale leaves for 1 minute.

3  Toss the kale, seeds and remaining salad ingredients together, then tip into your lunchbox.

4  Combine the dressing ingredients in a small jar or container with a tight-fitting lid. Season to taste.

5  Pour the dressing over the salad and toss well.

2 tablespoons sunflower kernels

2 tablespoons pumpkin seeds

1 tablespoon each hulled hemp seeds, sesame seeds and linseeds (flax seeds)

juice of ½ lemon

80 g (2¾ oz) baby kale leaves

¼ red onion, thinly sliced

handful of cherry tomatoes, halved

½ avocado, chopped

Lemon dressing
- 2 tablespoons extra virgin olive oil
- juice of ½ lemon

Raw kale on its own can be a little chewy, so here we soften it by massaging lemon into the leaves. This helps to change the texture, while the flavour and nutritional boost remain.

Grains & Seeds

# Beetroot & red quinoa salad

1 Toss the salad ingredients together, then tip into your lunchbox.

2 Combine the dressing ingredients in a small jar or container with a tight-fitting lid. Season to taste.

3 Pour the dressing over the salad just before serving and toss well.

150 g (1 cup) cooked and cooled red quinoa

3 cooked yellow baby beetroot (beets), quartered

handful of roasted almonds, roughly chopped

50 g (1¾ oz) feta, crumbled

large handful of baby spinach leaves

handful of chopped parsley leaves

Creamy dill dressing
- 1 tablespoon mayonnaise
- 1 tablespoon plain yoghurt
- juice of ½ lemon
- handful of finely chopped dill
- 1 tablespoon extra virgin olive oil

If yellow beetroot is not available, simply replace it with the more common red variety. Also, feel free to swap out the red quinoa with white or black quinoa.

Grains & Seeds

# Kimchi
# rice salad

1  Toss the salad ingredients
together, then tip into your
lunchbox.

2  Combine the dressing
ingredients in a small jar or
container with a tight-fitting lid.

3  Pour the dressing over the
salad just before serving
and toss well.

150 g (1 cup) cooked and cooled
brown rice

100 g (3½ oz) kimchi

2 tablespoons toasted sesame
seeds

handful of bean sprouts

handful of coriander (cilantro)
leaves

½ short cucumber, sliced

Sesame & ginger dressing
–  1 tablespoon rice wine vinegar
–  1 tablespoon soy sauce or tamari
–  1 teaspoon minced ginger
–  ½ teaspoon sesame oil

This healthy, moreish salad is a variation on kimchi fried rice. Here we use brown rice, a whole grain, which is rich in fibre and has a nuttier taste than white rice.

Grains & Seeds

# Couscous salad with left-over roast veg

1 Toss the salad ingredients together, then tip into your lunchbox.

2 Combine the dressing ingredients in a small jar or container with a tight-fitting lid. Season to taste.

3 Pour the dressing over the salad just before serving and toss well.

150 g (1 cup) cooked and cooled couscous

150 g (5½ oz) left-over roast vegetables

1 large handful of chopped mixed herbs, such as parsley, mint and dill

¼ red onion, finely chopped

Lemon dressing
- 2 tablespoons extra virgin olive oil
- juice of ½ lemon

This salad is the perfect option for the day after you've roasted up a big batch of colourful vegetables for dinner. Any vegetable at hand will work here – so toss in whatever you like.

Grains & Seeds

# Quick tabbouleh

1 Blitz the tomato in a food processor or blender until smooth.

2 Place the bulgur in a jar or container with a tight-fitting lid. Stir through 80 ml (⅓ cup) of the puréed tomato, along with the oil and lemon juice. Season to taste and seal the lid.

3 Add the remaining salad ingredients to your lunchbox.

4 Before serving, fluff the bulgur with a fork then add to the salad. Toss well.

1 large tomato

45 g (¼ cup) fine bulgur

2 teaspoons extra virgin olive oil

juice of ½ lemon

2 spring (green) onions, thinly sliced

large handful of mint leaves, finely chopped

large handful of parsley, finely chopped

flatbread, to serve

This salad is a freshness explosion, thanks to the abundance of parsley and mint – the real stars of this dish. For an even quicker option, swap out the bulgur for 100 g (⅔ cup) cooked instant couscous.

Grains & Seeds

# Peanutty rice & baby kale salad

1. Massage the lime juice into the baby kale leaves for 1 minute.

2. Toss the kale and remaining salad ingredients together, then tip into your lunchbox.

3. Combine the dressing ingredients in a small jar or container with a tight-fitting lid.

4. Pour the dressing over the salad just before serving and toss well.

juice of ½ lime

80 g (2¾ oz) roughly chopped baby kale

150 g (1 cup) cooked and cooled brown rice

1 spring (green) onion, sliced

2 tablespoons roughly chopped roasted unsalted peanuts

handful of shredded carrot

handful of coriander (cilantro) leaves

Peanut dressing
- 3 tablespoons peanut butter
- 1½ tablespoons rice wine vinegar
- 1 teaspoon toasted sesame oil
- juice of ½ lime

If you like the flavour and crunch of peanuts, you'll love this hearty salad. Choose a good-quality peanut butter for the dressing – one without added sugar – for the best outcome.

Grains & Seeds

# Quinoa & black bean salad with chipotle crema

1 Toss the salad ingredients together, then tip into your lunchbox.

2 Combine the dressing ingredients in a small jar or container with a tight-fitting lid. Season to taste.

3 Pour the dressing over the salad just before serving and toss well.

100 g (⅔ cup) cooked and cooled quinoa

100 g (3½ oz) drained tinned black beans

¼ green bell pepper (capsicum), finely diced

2 spring (green) onions, thinly sliced

½ avocado, diced

handful of coriander (cilantro) leaves

Chipotle crema dressing
- ½ chipotle chilli in adobo sauce, chopped
- juice of ½ lime
- 2 tablespoons mayonnaise

This salad uses the classic combination of black beans, avocado, coriander and chipotle. Tins of chipotle chillies in adobo sauce can be found in most supermarkets, or speciality stores.

# Red quinoa & pomegranate salad

1 Toss the salad ingredients together, then tip into your lunchbox.

2 Combine the dressing ingredients in a small jar or container with a tight-fitting lid. Season to taste.

3 Pour the dressing over the salad just before serving and toss well.

½ avocado, diced

150 g (1 cup) cooked and cooled red quinoa

1 celery stalk, thinly sliced

handful of pomegranate seeds

50 g (1¾ oz) feta, crumbled

handful of roughly chopped cashews

handful of mint leaves

Lemon garlic dressing
- 2 tablespoons extra virgin olive oil
- juice of ½ lemon
- ½ teaspoon minced garlic
- ½ teaspoon ground cumin
- pinch of caster (superfine) sugar

Pomegranate seeds give a pop of flavour with every mouthful in this salad. Cashews are there for added texture and flavour, but can be replaced with roasted almonds or pistachios if preferred.

Grains & Seeds

# Basmati rice & pea salad

1 Blanch the peas in boiling water for 1–2 minutes. Drain and refresh under cold running water.

2 Toss the peas and remaining salad ingredients together, then tip into your lunchbox.

3 Combine the dressing ingredients in a small jar or container with a tight-fitting lid. Season to taste.

4 Pour the dressing over the salad just before serving and toss well.

80 g (½ cup) frozen peas

150 g (1 cup) cooked and cooled basmati rice

1 celery stalk, thinly sliced

2 tablespoons sultanas (golden raisins)

handful of coriander (cilantro) leaves

2 spring (green) onions, thinly sliced

handful of slivered almonds

Ginger cumin dressing
- 2 tablespoons extra virgin olive oil
- juice of ½ lemon
- 1 teaspoon minced ginger
- 1 teaspoon ground cumin

This simple salad combines the crunch of celery and almonds, sweetness of sultanas and fresh flavours of pea and coriander on a bed of rice. The dressing is a perfect match for this dish.

Grains & Seeds

# Chia granola with berries

1 Toss the granola ingredients together, then tip into your lunchbox.

2 Combine the maple yoghurt ingredients in a small jar or container with a tight-fitting lid.

3 Spoon the maple yoghurt over the granola just before serving.

3 tablespoons black chia seeds

1 tablespoon sunflower kernels

handful of coconut flakes

75 g (¾ cup) toasted granola

handful of mint leaves

4 strawberries, hulled and halved

handful of blueberries

handful of raspberries

Maple yoghurt
- 90 g (⅓ cup) coconut yoghurt
- 1 tablespoon maple syrup

Not all coconut yoghurts are created equal.
Some are overloaded with sugar and too many
ingredients, so look out for a good-quality,
delicious-tasting one.

Grains & Seeds

Beans & Le
Beans &
Beans & Le
Beans & L
Beans & L
Beans &
Beans & L
Beans &
Beans &

Legumes
Legumes
Legumes
Legumes
Legumes
Legumes

# Middle Eastern bean salad

1 Toss the salad ingredients together. Season to taste, then tip into your lunchbox.

2 Combine the dressing ingredients in a small jar or container with a tight-fitting lid.

3 Pour the dressing over the salad just before serving and toss well.

150 g (5½ oz) drained tinned four-bean mix

½ short cucumber, sliced

2 handfuls of baby spinach leaves

2 tablespoons dried cranberries

Pomegranate dressing
- 1½ tablespoons extra virgin olive oil
- 1½ tablespoons lemon juice
- 1 tablespoon diced red onion
- 2 teaspoons pomegranate molasses
- 1 teaspoon za'atar spice mix

Here you'll find a healthy mixture of beans and salad greens, with the sweetness of dried cranberries – also sold as 'craisins'.

Beans & Legumes

# Sicilian olive, tuna & cannellini bean salad

1   Toss the salad ingredients together. Season to taste, then tip into your lunchbox.

2   Combine the dressing ingredients in a small jar or container with a tight-fitting lid.

3   Pour the dressing over the salad just before serving and toss well.

95 g (3¼ oz) tin tuna in chilli oil, drained

100 g (3½ oz) drained tinned cannellini beans

small handful of pitted Sicilian green olives

2 handfuls of mixed salad greens

Parsley & caper dressing
–   1½ tablespoons extra virgin olive oil
–   zest and juice of ½ lemon
–   1 tablespoon chopped parsley
–   1 teaspoon baby capers

Drawing inspiration from Italy, this salad is a breeze to put together. If you prefer yours without spice, go for tinned tuna in olive oil instead of one infused with chilli.

Beans & Legumes

# Chorizo, pepper & borlotti bean salad

1 Toss the salad ingredients together. Season to taste, then tip into your lunchbox.

2 Combine the dressing ingredients in a small jar or container with a tight-fitting lid.

3 Pour the dressing over the salad just before serving and toss well.

150 g (5½ oz) drained tinned borlotti (cranberry) beans

80 g (2¾ oz) smoked chorizo, sliced

2 marinated roasted red bell peppers (capsicums), sliced

2 handfuls of rocket (arugula)

Parsley & paprika dressing
- 1½ tablespoons extra virgin olive oil
- 1½ tablespoons Spanish sherry vinegar
- 1 tablespoon chopped parsley leaves
- ½ teaspoon smoked paprika

Chorizo is the star of this deliciously tasty and hearty Spanish-inspired salad. Dry, or smoked chorizo, such as the one called for here, can be eaten without any cooking or preparation.

Beans & Legumes

# Spicy black bean & quinoa salad

1   Toss the salad ingredients together. Season to taste, then tip into your lunchbox.

2   Combine the dressing ingredients in a small jar or container with a tight-fitting lid.

3   Pour the dressing over the salad just before serving and toss well.

100 g (3½ oz) drained tinned black beans

150 g (1 cup) cooked and cooled quinoa

handful of cherry tomatoes, halved

½ avocado, diced

Spicy jalapeño dressing
–   1 tablespoon extra virgin olive oil
–   1 tablespoon lime juice
–   1 teaspoon green Tabasco or other green jalapeño sauce

Quinoa comes in red, white and black varieties – sometimes mixed together and sold as tricolour quinoa – but any type will work here.

Beans & Legumes

# Lentil, ricotta & beetroot salad

1   Toss the salad ingredients together. Season to taste, then tip into your lunchbox.

2   Combine the dressing ingredients in a small jar or container with a tight-fitting lid.

3   Pour the dressing over the salad just before serving and toss well.

150 g (⅔ cup) drained tinned lentils

handful of radicchio leaves, torn

100 g (3½ oz) raw yellow beetroot (beet), very thinly sliced

50 g (1¾ oz) ricotta, crumbled

White balsamic dressing
–   2 tablespoons extra virgin olive oil
–   1½ tablespoons white balsamic vinegar
–   1 teaspoon dijon mustard
–   1 teaspoon honey

A treat for the eyes, this beautiful, colourful salad hums with delicious, fresh flavours. Yellow or golden beetroot isn't always easy to find – but can be simply replaced with regular red beetroot.

Beans & Legumes

# Crunchy greens & lentil salad

1 Toss the salad ingredients together. Season to taste, then tip into your lunchbox.

2 Combine the dressing ingredients in a small jar or container with a tight-fitting lid.

3 Pour the dressing over the salad just before serving and toss well.

150 g (⅔ cup) drained tinned lentils

100 g (3½ oz) sugar snap peas, blanched

3 broccolini stems, blanched, cut into 5 cm (2 in) lengths

handful of baby spinach leaves

Sesame & ginger dressing
- 1 tablespoon rice wine vinegar
- 1 tablespoon soy sauce or tamari
- 1 teaspoon minced ginger
- ½ teaspoon sesame oil

There's nothing like the satisfying crunch of a healthy salad. Here, it's the sugar snap peas that provide that delicious textural bite!

Beans & Legumes

# Chicken, lentil & caper salad

1   Toss the salad ingredients together. Season to taste, then tip into your lunchbox.

2   Combine the dressing ingredients in a small jar or container with a tight-fitting lid.

3   Pour the dressing over the salad just before serving and toss well.

150 g (⅔ cup) drained tinned lentils

100 g (3½ oz) shredded cooked chicken

large handful of mixed small heirloom tomatoes, halved

handful of baby capers

Preserved lemon & honey dressing
- ¼ preserved lemon, rind only, finely chopped
- juice of ½ lemon
- 1 teaspoon honey
- 1½ teaspoons dijon mustard
- 2 tablespoons extra virgin olive oil

Here's a great use for left-over chicken – which could be roast or poached chicken, or even store-bought barbecued chicken. To shred the chicken, use two forks or clean hands to pull it apart.

Beans & Legumes

# Chickpea, carrot & dill salad

1 Toss the salad ingredients together. Season to taste, then tip into your lunchbox.

2 Combine the dressing ingredients in a small jar or container with a tight-fitting lid.

3 Pour the dressing over the salad just before serving and toss well.

150 g (5½ oz) drained tinned chickpeas

large handful of shredded carrot

large handful of roughly chopped dill

1 celery stalk, thinly sliced

Lemon dressing
- 2 tablespoons extra virgin olive oil
- juice of ½ lemon

This vegan salad is super quick to put together. To save even more time in the kitchen, buy pre-shredded carrot from the supermarket rather than shredding the carrot yourself.

Beans & Legumes

# Spicy black-eyed bean, corn & coriander salad

1. Toss the salad ingredients together. Season to taste, then tip into your lunchbox.

2. Combine the dressing ingredients in a small jar or container with a tight-fitting lid.

3. Pour the dressing over the salad just before serving and toss well.

150 g (5½ oz) drained tinned black-eyed beans

¼ red bell pepper (capsicum), finely diced

75 g (2¾ oz) drained tinned sweet corn kernels

large handful of coriander (cilantro) leaves

Jalapeño yoghurt dressing
- 2 tablespoons Greek yoghurt
- juice of 1 lime
- 1 tablespoon finely chopped pickled jalapeños

Black-eyed beans have an earthy, nutty flavour that combines well with the other ingredients in this salad. If you find the tinned version hard to come by, simply replace them with black beans.

Beans & Legumes

# Lentil, haloumi & herb salad

1 Toss the salad ingredients together, then tip into your lunchbox.

2 Combine the dressing ingredients in a small jar or container with a tight-fitting lid. Season to taste.

3 Pour the dressing over the salad just before serving and toss well.

50 g (1¾ oz) slice of haloumi, fried in hot oil for 3 minutes, cubed

150 g (⅔ cup) drained tinned brown lentils

1 tomato, diced

handful each of mint, parsley and coriander (cilantro), chopped

Lemon & cumin dressing
- juice of ½ lemon
- 1 teaspoon ground cumin
- 2 tablespoons extra virgin olive oil

The haloumi brings a wonderful savoury saltiness to this salad, but if you want to save a little time you can substitute ricotta salata (salted ricotta) – or even just some good-quality fresh ricotta.

Beans & Legumes

# Tuna, cannellini beans, goji & kale salad

1   Toss the salad ingredients together, then tip into your lunchbox.

2   Combine the dressing ingredients in a small jar or container with a tight-fitting lid. Season to taste.

3   Pour the dressing over the salad just before serving and toss well.

100 g (3½ oz) drained tinned cannellini beans

95 g (3¼ oz) tin tuna in oil, drained

3 tablespoons goji berries

handful of baby kale leaves

2 tablespoons grated parmesan

Cider vinegar dressing
- 1½ tablespoons apple cider vinegar
- ½ teaspoon dijon mustard
- ½ teaspoon honey
- 2 tablespoons extra virgin olive oil

Use baby kale for this recipe, as the larger leaves can be a little tough and bitter to eat raw. If unavailable, you can substitute any green leafy vegetable, such as baby spinach leaves.

Beans & Legumes

# Black bean nacho salad

1 Place the tortilla chips in an airtight container.

2 Toss the remaining salad ingredients together with ½ teaspoon of salt, then tip into your lunchbox.

3 Combine the dressing ingredients in a small jar or container with a tight-fitting lid. Season to taste.

4 Pour the dressing over the salad just before serving and use the tortilla chips to scoop up the bean mixture.

50 g (1¾ oz) tortilla chips

150 g (5½ oz) drained tinned black beans

75 g (2¾ oz) drained tinned sweet corn kernels

2 spring onions (scallions), thinly sliced

½ green bell pepper (capsicum), diced

juice of ½ lime

handful of coriander (cilantro) leaves, chopped

Chipotle dressing
- ¼ teaspoon minced garlic
- 2 teaspoons chipotle in adobo hot sauce
- juice of ½ lime
- 2 tablespoons sour cream

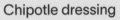

This salad is just like eating a bowl of nachos –
but without the grease! Look for good-quality
tortilla chips at Latin grocers or in the Mexican
section of your supermarket.

Beans & Legumes

# Lentil, beetroot & feta salad

1   Toss the salad ingredients together, then tip into your lunchbox.

2   Combine the dressing ingredients in a small jar or container with a tight-fitting lid. Season to taste.

3   Pour the dressing over the salad just before serving and toss well.

4 cooked baby beetroot (beets), quartered

1 short cucumber, halved lengthways and sliced

150 g (⅔ cup) drained tinned brown lentils

30 g (1 oz) feta, crumbled

handful each of mint and baby spinach leaves

Balsamic dressing
-   1 tablespoon balsamic vinegar
-   1 teaspoon dijon mustard
-   2 tablespoons extra virgin olive oil

Pre-cooked beetroot is available in vacuum-sealed packs from the supermarket. Look for varieties with no added sugar or preservatives.

Beans & Legumes

# Tuna, chickpea & caper salad

1 Toss the salad ingredients together, then tip into your lunchbox.

2 Combine the dressing ingredients in a small jar or container with a tight-fitting lid. Season to taste.

3 Pour the dressing over the salad just before serving and toss well.

95 g (3¼ oz) tin tuna in oil, drained

100 g (3½ oz) drained tinned chickpeas (garbanzo beans)

¼ red onion, thinly sliced

2 tablespoons finely grated parmesan

large handful of shredded iceberg lettuce

1 tablespoon baby capers

1 tablespoon chopped dill

Red wine vinegar dressing
- 1 tablespoon red wine vinegar
- 2 tablespoons extra virgin olive oil

The sweet and salty capers take this salad to another level. Feel free to throw in any herbs you have on hand to add some more colour to this hearty salad.

Beans & Legumes

# Lentil, zucchini & mint salad

1 Combine the zucchini, lemon juice and a pinch of salt in a bowl. Use your hands to massage the lemon juice into the zucchini. Add the remaining salad ingredients, then tip into your lunchbox.

2 Combine the dressing ingredients in a small jar or container with a tight-fitting lid. Season to taste.

3 Pour the dressing over the salad just before serving and toss well.

1 zucchini (courgette), cut into ribbons using a vegetable peeler

juice of ½ lemon

150 g (⅔ cup) drained tinned brown lentils

small handful of parsley, chopped

large handful of mint leaves, larger leaves chopped

30 g (1 oz) feta, crumbled

2 tablespoons seeds, such as sunflower and pumpkin seeds

Lemon dressing
- zest and juice of ½ lemon
- 1 teaspoon white wine vinegar
- 2 tablespoons extra virgin olive oil

You can try goat's cheese in this recipe instead of the feta. You can also mix up the herbs and use whatever you have in your fridge or growing on your balcony or in your backyard.

Beans & Legumes

# Cannellini bean & feta salad

1   Toss the salad ingredients together, then tip into your lunchbox.

2   Combine the dressing ingredients in a small jar or container with a tight-fitting lid. Season to taste.

3   Pour the dressing over the salad just before serving and toss well.

150 g (5½ oz) drained tinned cannellini beans

¼ red onion, thinly sliced

large handful of grape (baby plum) tomatoes

small handful of parsley, roughly chopped

50 g (⅓ cup) feta, crumbled

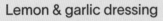

Lemon & garlic dressing
–   ½ teaspoon minced garlic
–   juice of ½ lemon
–   2 teaspoons apple cider vinegar
–   1½ tablespoons extra virgin olive oil

This is a simple salad that really delivers on flavour. You can use butter (lima) beans or even chickpeas (garbanzo beans) instead of the cannellini beans.

Beans & Legumes

# Mexican rice & bean salad

1 Toss the salad ingredients together, then tip into your lunchbox.

2 Combine the dressing ingredients in a small jar or container with a tight-fitting lid. Season to taste.

3 Pour the dressing over the salad just before serving and toss well.

100 g (3½ oz) drained tinned kidney beans

120 g (4½ oz) cooked and cooled Mexican rice

75 g (2¾ oz) drained tinned sweet corn kernels

¼ red onion, finely chopped

¼ red bell pepper (capsicum), finely chopped

handful of coriander (cilantro) leaves

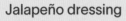

Jalapeño dressing
- 3–4 pickled jalapeño slices, finely chopped
- juice of 1 lime
- 2 tablespoons yoghurt

Instant Mexican rice is available in packets in most supermarkets – you'll want to stock up once you taste this salad. If you're not a fan of spice, feel free to omit the jalapeños from the dressing.

Beans & Legumes

# Kale & chickpea caesar

1 Massage the lemon juice and nutritional yeast into the kale leaves for 1 minute.

2 Toss the kale and remaining salad ingredients together, then tip into your lunchbox.

3 Combine the dressing ingredients in a small jar or container with a tight-fitting lid. Season to taste.

4 Pour the dressing over the salad just before serving and toss well.

½ lemon

1 tablespoon nutritional yeast

4 large kale leaves, roughly chopped

150 g (5½ oz) drained tinned chickpeas

50 g (1⅔ cups) croutons

small handful of crispy-fried shallots

Caper mayo dressing
- 2 tablespoons vegan mayonnaise
- juice of ½ lemon
- 1 teaspoon vegan dijon mustard
- 2 teaspoons capers, chopped

This plant-based variation on the classic caesar salad is every bit as delicious – and so much quicker to prepare – as the original.

Beans & Legumes

# Lentil, pear & blue cheese salad

1 Combine the pear and lemon juice in a bowl and toss to combine.

2 Toss the pear and remaining salad ingredients together, then tip into your lunchbox.

3 Combine the dressing ingredients in a small jar or container with a tight-fitting lid. Season to taste.

4 Pour the dressing over the salad just before serving and toss well.

1 pear, cored and sliced

juice of ½ lemon

150 g (⅔ cup) drained tinned lentils

handful of chopped hazelnuts

large handful of rocket (arugula)

50 g (1¾ oz) blue cheese, crumbled

Sweet balsamic dressing
- 1½ tablespoons balsamic vinegar
- 1 teaspoon maple syrup
- 1 teaspoon dijon mustard
- 2 tablespoons extra virgin olive oil

There are so many great vegan cheeses available, so try using vegan blue cheese for this recipe. The hazelnuts add a nutty, earthy flavour – but feel free to swap them with any other nuts.

Beans & Legumes

# Falafel salad

1 Place the pita chips in an airtight container.

2 Toss the remaining salad ingredients together, then tip into your lunchbox.

3 Combine the dressing ingredients with 1 tablespoon of water in a small jar or container with a tight-fitting lid. Season to taste.

4 Pour the dressing over the salad just before serving and toss well. Use the pita chips to scoop up the salad.

handful of pita crisps, store-bought or made with pita bread

3–4 falafel balls, roughly torn

handful of cherry tomatoes, halved

large handful of parsley

1 short cucumber, chopped

Tahini dressing
- 1 teaspoon minced garlic
- 2 tablespoons tahini
- juice of ½ lemon

To make pita crisps, cut a pita bread into pieces, spray with olive oil, sprinkle with spices and bake in a moderate oven for about 10 minutes, until crisp and golden. Cool and store in an airtight container until you're ready to use them.

Beans & Legumes

# White bean & feta salad

1. Use a vegetable peeler to cut the cucumber into ribbons. Toss together with the remaining salad ingredients, then tip into your lunchbox.

2. Combine the dressing ingredients in a small jar or container with a tight-fitting lid. Season to taste.

3. Pour the dressing over the salad just before serving.

1 short cucumber

150 g (5½ oz) drained tinned cannellini beans

80 g (2¾ oz) feta, crumbled

¼ small red onion, thinly sliced

small handful of mint leaves

Preserved lemon & sumac dressing
- ¼ preserved lemon, rind only, finely chopped
- ½ teaspoon ground sumac
- ½ teaspoon minced garlic
- 1 tablespoon red wine vinegar
- 2 tablespoons extra virgin olive oil

Cannellini beans are a creamy, mild-tasting legume that love to soak up the flavours around them. You can swap out the cannellini beans for another kind, such as kidney or borlotti (cranberry) beans.

Beans & Legumes

# Sugar snap
# & apple slaw

1   Blanch the sugar snap peas
    in boiling water for 1 minute.
    Drain and refresh under cold
    running water.

2   Toss the sugar snap peas and
    remaining salad ingredients
    together, then tip into your
    lunchbox.

3   Blitz the dressing ingredients in a
    small food processor or blender
    until smooth. Season to taste and
    transfer to a small jar or container
    with a tight-fitting lid.

4   Spoon the dressing over the
    salad just before serving and
    toss well.

150 g (5½ oz) sugar snap peas

handful of finely shredded red
cabbage

2 tablespoons toasted walnuts,
chopped

1 small green apple, spiralised

Avocado dressing
–   ½ avocado
–   2 tablespoons sour cream or yoghurt
–   1 tablespoon chopped coriander (cilantro)
–   juice of ½ lime

If you're short on time – and want to save the one minute of blanching time – feel free to swap out the sugar snap peas for snow peas (mangetout), which don't require any cooking at all.

Beans & Legumes

# Pea, pomegranate & fig salad

1 Blanch the peas in boiling water for 1–2 minutes. Drain and refresh under cold running water.

2 Toss the peas and remaining salad ingredients together, then tip into your lunchbox.

3 Combine the dressing ingredients in a small jar or container with a tight-fitting lid. Season to taste.

4 Pour the dressing over the salad just before serving and toss well.

120 g (¾ cup) frozen peas

80 g (⅓ cup) drained tinned lentils

2 figs, quartered

2 tablespoons pomegranate seeds

large handful of rocket (arugula)

small handful of chopped toasted macadamia nuts

Pomegranate dressing
- 2 tablespoons extra virgin olive oil
- 1 tablespoon pomegranate molasses
- juice of ½ lemon
- 1 teaspoon maple syrup

Look out for pomegranate seeds sold separately in sealed punnets or in frozen packets in your supermarket, to save the time of seeding the fruit yourself.

Beans & Legumes

# Black bean & edamame salad

1 Toss the salad ingredients together, then tip into your lunchbox.

2 Combine the dressing ingredients in a small jar or container with a tight-fitting lid.

3 Pour the dressing over the salad just before serving and toss well.

100 g (3½ oz) cooked edamame beans

80 g (2¾ oz) drained tinned black beans

3–4 radishes, chopped

1 short cucumber, chopped

1 sheet of nori, halved, then thinly sliced

1 tablespoon toasted sesame seeds

Soy maple dressing
- 2 tablespoons soy sauce
- 1 tablespoon rice wine vinegar
- 2 teaspoons mirin
- 2 teaspoons maple syrup
- 1 teaspoon sesame oil

Edamame beans, or soy beans, can be found in the frozen section of supermarkets and are available whole or pre-podded. They make a delicious snack on their own, sprinkled with sea salt.

Beans & Legumes

# Chickpea, avocado & feta salad

1 Toss the salad ingredients together, then tip into your lunchbox.

2 Combine the dressing ingredients in a small jar or container with a tight-fitting lid. Season to taste.

3 Pour the dressing over the salad just before serving and toss well.

150 g (5½ oz) drained tinned chickpeas

½ avocado, diced

50 g (1¾ oz) feta, diced

¼ red onion, finely diced

handful of chopped coriander (cilantro)

Lime dressing
- 2 tablespoons extra virgin olive oil
- juice of 1 lime

This hearty chickpea salad combines the rich, creamy flavour of avocado and feta with the tanginess of lime and pungency of coriander. A delicious – and filling – lunchtime combination!

Beans & Legumes

# Black bean chopped salad

1 Toss the salad ingredients together, then tip into your lunchbox.

2 Combine the dressing ingredients in a small jar or container with a tight-fitting lid.

3 Pour the dressing over the salad just before serving and toss well.

150 g (5½ oz) drained tinned black beans

2–3 leaves each of radicchio and cos (romaine) lettuce, chopped

1 celery stalk, thinly sliced

¼ small red onion, finely diced

small handful of cherry tomatoes, quartered

small handful of chopped parsley

small handful of dried cranberries

Dijon dressing
- 2 tablespoons extra virgin olive oil
- 1 tablespoon red wine vinegar
- 2 teaspoons dijon mustard

This salad is a great combination of flavour, colour and texture. If you prefer, swap the parsley for coriander (cilantro) and cranberries for raisins or currants.

Beans & Legumes

# Lentil, radish & herb salad

1 Toss the salad ingredients together, then tip into your lunchbox.

2 Combine the dressing ingredients in a small jar or container with a tight-fitting lid. Season to taste.

3 Pour the dressing over the salad just before serving and toss well.

150 g (⅔ cup) drained tinned lentils

3 radishes, very thinly sliced

handful each of rocket (arugula), mint and parsley leaves

1 tomato, diced

Lemon & cumin dressing
- juice of ½ lemon
- 1 teaspoon ground cumin
- 2 tablespoons extra virgin olive oil

There are many types of lentils available, which are chiefly categorised by their colour – brown, green, red, yellow and black. This simple recipe will work with whatever lentils you have at hand.

Beans & Legumes

Bento
Bento
Bento
Bento

Boxes

Boxes

Boxes

Boxes

Boxes

150 g (5½ oz/1 cup) cooked and cooled rice

100 g (3½ oz) cooked edamame beans

60 g (2 oz) store-bought seaweed salad

100 g (3½ oz) sashimi-grade raw salmon, sliced

condiments such as soy sauce, pickled ginger and wasabi paste

1 Place all the ingredients in your bento lunchbox and seal.

# Japanese bento

This bento is best put together using fresh, sashimi-grade salmon. Fishmongers can help you out here – as well as pre-slicing the fish. Seaweed salad is readily available in Japanese supermarkets, delis and even some sushi shops.

4 baguette slices, toasted

60 g (2 oz) brie

handful of grapes

small handful of cornichons

100 g (3½ oz) chicken liver pâté

1   Place all the ingredients in your bento lunchbox and seal.

# French bento

Take a quick trip to Paris with this French-inspired bento box. Go for a good-quality pâté, as it's really the star of this lunch.

60 g (2 oz) salami

handful of taralli rings, grissini or sliced focaccia

1 burrata

handful of cherry tomatoes, halved

3 tablespoons store-bought basil pesto

1   Place all the ingredients in your bento lunchbox and seal.

# Italian bento

Burrata is a cream-filled mozzarella cheese ball. It's addictively delicious and rich – and the perfect accompaniment to the other ingredients in this Italian-inspired bento. If you prefer, however, feel free to replace the burrata with a fresh mozzarella ball instead – it'll be a little less messy!

1 small pita bread, sliced into wedges

4 dolmades

80 g (2¾ oz) pickled octopus

50 g (1¾ oz) marinated feta, cubed

handful of marinated kalamata olives

1  Place all the ingredients in your bento lunchbox and seal.

# Hellenic bento

The ingredients in this bento are all easy to find at the deli counter of most supermarkets or specialist Greek (or Italian) stores. If you like, include a lemon wedge for squeezing over before diving in.

rye bread slices

2 boiled eggs

75 g (2½ oz) smoked fish

red onion slices

40 g (1½ oz) cream cheese
or crème fraîche

1 Place all the ingredients in your
bento lunchbox and seal.

# Nordic bento

A nod to Scandinavia with this winning combination
of smoked fish, cream cheese and rye bread.
Smoked fish can be found in most supermarkets –
or in more varieties at specialist delis.

Bento Boxes

4 tablespoons avocado dip

handful of beetroot (beet) or veggie crackers

100 g (3½ oz) vegetable crudités

60 g (2 oz) vegan cashew cheese

handful of tamari nuts or goji berry nut trail mix

1   Place all the ingredients in your bento lunchbox and seal.

# Vegan bento

This satisfyingly healthy bento delivers on taste and crunchiness. Cashew cheese and avocado dip are available in supermarkets, food markets and specialist retailers, but are easy to make as well, if you prefer.

pumpernickel bread slices, spread with mustard

80 g (2¾ oz) sliced pastrami

3 tablespoons beetroot (beet) sauerkraut

2 dill pickles, sliced

150 g (½ cup) store-bought potato salad

1 Place all the ingredients in your bento lunchbox and seal.

# NY deli bento

Take a trip to New York from the comfort of your lunchtime bento! Pastrami is a classic NY deli meat made from beef. There are different styles and qualities of pastrami available – so shop around and find the most delicious variety you can.

2 hard-boiled eggs

1 English muffin, split, toasted and buttered

1 tomato, sliced

½ avocado, sliced

50 g (1¾ oz) double-smoked ham, sliced

1  Place all the ingredients in your bento lunchbox and seal.

# All-day breakfast bento

Hard-boiled eggs are a great addition to a bento box – adding flavour and protein. If you prefer to save time when putting your bento together, cook your eggs and store in the fridge for up to a week.

2 small pita breads, cut into triangles

3 tablespoons tzatziki

50 g (1¾ oz) feta, chopped

handful of pitted kalamata olives

1 tomato, roughly chopped

½ short cucumber, chopped

¼ red bell pepper (capsicum), chopped

extra virgin olive oil, for drizzling

1 Place the pita bread, tzatziki and feta into seperate compartments in your bento box

2 Combine the olives, tomato, cucumber and capsicum in a small bowl and drizzle with olive oil and place in the remaining compartment.

# Greek salad bento

This recipe is a classic combination loved around the world. Separating the ingredients ensures the freshness is retained when you dive in at lunchtime.

60 g (¼ cup) coconut yoghurt

handful of purple tortilla chips

2 mini capsicums (bell peppers)

60 g (¼ cup) hummus

25 g (1 oz) dark vegan chocolate

handful of mixed nuts and seeds of your choice

# Protein bento

1   Place the yoghurt and tortilla chips into seperate compartments in your bento box.

2   Slice the tops off the mini capsicums and scoop out the seeds. Spoon the hummus into the capsicum shells.

3   Place the capsicums, chocolate and nuts into the remaining bento compartments.

This is the perfect bento when you need an energy boost. Hollowed-out mini capsicums make the perfect vessel for hummus, or any dip – so feel free to replace the hummus with another dip.

267

60 g (2 oz) watermelon, sliced into small wedges

handful of cherries

handful of coconut flakes

60 g (¼ cup) coconut yoghurt

2 teaspoons maple syrup

½ red dragonfruit, peeled and chopped

1 Divide the fruit and coconut flakes among the compartments in your bento box.

2 Combine the coconut yoghurt and maple syrup in a small container, then place in the bento.

# Summer fruit salad bento

This is a simple, nutrient-boosting salad which is a perfect light choice for the summer months. Swap out any of the fruit for whatever is in season and at its best.

Bento Boxes

- 100 g (⅔ cup) cooked and cooled brown rice

- 2 spring (green) onions, sliced

- handful of bean sprouts

- handful of shredded carrot

- 1 tablespoon dark soy sauce

- 1 teaspoon sesame oil

- 6 cos (romaine) lettuce leaves

- handful of roughly chopped roasted peanuts

# San choy bau bento

1. Combine the rice, spring onion, bean sprouts, carrot, soy sauce and sesame oil and place in a compartment in your bento box.

2. Place the lettuce and peanuts in separate compartments in your bento box.

3. To eat, spoon the rice into the lettuce and top with the peanuts.

San choy bau is an iconic Cantonese dish, with many variations. This vegan interpretation combines flavoursome rice with crunchy peanuts encased in crisp lettuce leaves – a perfect, interactive lunch!

3 tablespoons store-bought soba dipping sauce

180 g (6½ oz) instant soba noodles

50 g (1¾ oz) podded edamame beans

handful of cherry tomatoes, halved

½ avocado, sliced

1   Pour the dipping sauce into a small jar or container with a tight-fitting lid.

2   Cook the soba and edamame separately in boiling water for 2 minutes. Drain and rinse under cold running water.

3   Place the soba and edamame into your bento. Divide the remaining ingredients among the compartments.

4   To eat, dip the soba into the sauce, or tip all the ingredients into a bowl and toss to make a salad.

# Soba bento

Cold soba dishes are loved in Japan, where this bento has its inspiration. Bring along a pair of chopsticks and dip your noodles into the sauce for a satisfying lunch.

sliced crusty bread

60 g (¼ cup) store-bought rocket pesto

handful of cherry tomatoes, halved

3 marinated artichokes, quartered

2 slices of marinated eggplant (aubergine), sliced

1 roasted red capsicum (bell pepper), sliced

handful of baby spinach leaves

# Antipasto bento

1 Place the pesto in a small jar or container with a tight-fitting lid, then transfer to your bento box along with the bread.

2 Combine the tomatoes, artichoke, eggplant, capsicum and spinach. Place the salad mix into the bento.

4 When ready to eat, smear the pesto onto the crusty bread and top with some of the salad mixture.

You can mix up the ingredients with whatever antipasti you might have at home. Try adding cured meats, olives, feta or marinated mushrooms.

274

100 g (3½ oz) kimchi

2 toasted nori sheets,
cut into squares

3 tablespoons mayonnaise

1 carrot, cut into batons

½ cucumber, cut into batons

100 g (⅔ cup) cooked and
cooled brown rice

soy sauce, for dipping
(optional)

1  Place the ingredients in separate
   compartments in your bento box.

2  To eat, spoon a little mayo over a
   nori square and spread some rice
   and kimchi over the top.

3  Top with carrot and cucumber,
   then roll up. Dip into soy sauce
   if you like.

# Korean sushi bento

This bento is a do-it-yourself sushi kit for lunchtime!
There are many varieties of kimchi available, so look
for one that suits you best.

Wraps

Wraps

Wraps

Wraps

Wraps

Wraps

Wraps

Wraps

Wraps

Wraps

# Smoked chicken ranch wrap

Smoked chicken breast is a great choice if you want to add some delicious smoky flavour to your salad. You can buy it from butchers, delis and supermarkets.

1   Top the wrap with all the ingredients.

2   Roll up and secure the wrap.

1 wrap

handful of roughly torn cos (romaine) lettuce

100 g (3½ oz) smoked chicken breast, diced

1 small celery stalk, diced

¼ avocado, sliced

Ranch mayo
- 2½ tablespoons mayonnaise
- 2 teaspoons buttermilk
- ¼ teaspoon minced garlic
- 1 teaspoon each chopped dill and chives

# Turkey, gruyère & kale wrap

The perfect lunchtime treat – a deliciously moreish wrap with turkey, apple, kale, cheese and a creamy dressing.

1  Top the wrap with all the ingredients.

2  Roll up and secure the wrap.

1 wrap

handful of finely shredded kale

¼ granny smith apple, julienned

4 slices honey-roasted turkey breast

30 g (1 oz) grated gruyère

Honey mustard mayo
–  2½ tablespoons mayonnaise
–  1 teaspoon dijon mustard
–  1 teaspoon honey

# Smoked salmon wrap

This wrap is a play on the classic smoked salmon bagel. Herbed cream cheese will keep in your fridge for at least a week – so you can whip it up on the weekend for the week of lunches ahead.

1 Spread the herbed cream cheese over the wrap.

2 Top the wrap with the remaining ingredients.

3 Roll up and secure the wrap.

1 wrap

handful of mixed baby greens

½ short cucumber, sliced into thin ribbons

70 g (2½ oz) smoked salmon

¼ red onion, thinly sliced

Herbed cream cheese
- 4 tablespoons cream cheese
- 1 tablespoon finely chopped herbs, such as chives, dill and parsley
- 1 teaspoon baby capers
- ½ teaspoon finely grated lemon zest

# Falafel wrap

Falafel wraps make a filling vegetarian lunch. Falafel balls can be bought from the supermarket or from falafel shops, and are usually made from chickpeas or broad (fava) beans – or a mixture of both.

1 Top the wrap with all the ingredients.

2 Roll up and secure the wrap.

1 wrap

3–4 falafel balls, roughly torn

handful of torn cos (romaine) lettuce

½ tomato, diced

some Turkish pickled turnips, chopped

Tahini yoghurt sauce
- 2 tablespoons Greek yoghurt
- 1 teaspoon tahini
- 1 teaspoon lemon juice
- 1 teaspoon finely chopped parsley
- ½ teaspoon minced garlic

# Green goddess wrap

Take a trip back to 1970s California, where the green goddess dressing was ubiquitous. A nutritious, delicious wrap in every bite.

1  Spread the hummus over the wrap.

2  Top the wrap with the remaining ingredients.

3  Roll up and secure the wrap.

3 tablespoons green hummus or regular hummus

1 spinach wrap

½ avocado, sliced

handful of baby spinach leaves

handful of alfalfa sprouts

Green goddess dressing
- 3 tablespoons Greek yoghurt
- 1 tablespoon finely chopped herbs, such as basil, tarragon and chives
- 1 teaspoon lemon juice
- ½ teaspoon dijon mustard

# Submarine wrap

This is a wrap version of a classic 'sub' roll that uses a selection of deli meats, cheese, tomato and lettuce. It packs all the flavour – but without the heaviness of so much bread!

1  Top the wrap with all the ingredients.

2  Roll up and secure the wrap.

1 wrap

3 slices each of mortadella, salami and ham

2 slices of provolone cheese

1 roma (plum) tomato, sliced

handful of shredded cos (romaine) lettuce

Italian vinaigrette
- 2 teaspoons extra virgin olive oil
- 1 teaspoon red wine vinegar
- ¼ teaspoon dried Italian herb mix

# Caprese wrap

Here, we tie up all the wonderful flavours of a classic Italian caprese salad in a handy wrap!

1   Top the wrap with all the ingredients.

2   Roll up and secure the wrap.

1 sun-dried tomato wrap

handful of rocket (arugula)

small handful of heirloom cherry tomatoes, sliced

½ fresh mozzarella ball, sliced

¼ red onion, thinly sliced

Pesto mayo dressing
- 2 tablespoons store-bought pesto
- 1 tablespoon mayonnaise
- 2 teaspoons lemon juice

292

# Chicken tandoori wrap

A delicious, tangy wrap with bursts of flavour from the fresh mango and yoghurt sauce. This also makes a great salad – replace the wrap with rice, mix it all together and stir in the sauce just before serving.

1 Toss the chicken in the tandoori yoghurt sauce.

2 Top the wrap with all the ingredients.

3 Roll up and secure the wrap

120 g (4½ oz) shredded cooked chicken

1 wrap

¼ small red onion, thinly sliced

¼ short cucumber, thinly sliced

¼ mango, sliced

Tandoori yoghurt sauce
- 2½ tablespoons Greek yoghurt
- 1 tablespoon finely chopped mint leaves
- 1 teaspoon tandoori paste
- 1 teaspoon lemon juice

# Mexican prawn caesar wrap

This recipe calls for cotija cheese – a hard, salty, cow's milk cheese originating in the town of Cotija, Mexico. If available, it's a great, authentic addition to this wrap. Otherwise, go for a crumbly feta instead.

1 Top the wrap with all the ingredients.

2 Roll up and secure the wrap.

1 wrap

handful of torn cos (romaine) lettuce

½ avocado, sliced

5–6 large cooked peeled prawns (shrimp)

2 tablespoons crumbled Mexican cotija cheese, or feta

Coriander caesar dressing
- 2½ tablespoons mayonnaise
- 1 tablespoon finely chopped coriander (cilantro) leaves
- 1 anchovy fillet, finely chopped
- 2 teaspoons lime juice
- ¼ teaspoon minced garlic

# Tahini chickpea salad wrap

With its brilliant combination of ingredients, this spinach wrap is a vegan equivalent of tuna salad. It has much of the flavour and texture of a tuna wrap, to satisfy any meat-eater.

1   Roughly mash the chickpeas in a bowl.

2   Mix in the celery and onion.

3   Top the wrap with all the ingredients.

4   Roll up and secure the wrap.

80 g (2¾ oz) drained tinned chickpeas

½ celery stalk, finely diced

¼ red onion, finely diced

1 spinach wrap

handful of mixed salad greens

Tahini sauce
–   1 tablespoon tahini
–   1 tablespoon lemon juice
–   ½ teaspoon minced baby capers
–   ½ teaspoon dijon mustard

# Festive turkey wrap

This wrap can be enjoyed any time of the year – but in holiday season, you can replace the sliced turkey breast with left-over roast turkey.

1 Spread the cream cheese over the wrap.

2 Top the wrap with the remaining ingredients.

3 Roll up and secure the wrap.

3 tablespoons cream cheese

1 wrap

1 tablespoon cranberry relish

handful of rocket (arugula) leaves

80 g (2¾ oz) sliced smoked turkey breast

1 tablespoon chopped honey-spiced pecans

# Crunchy rainbow wrap

Here's a wrap bursting with colour, flavour and vitality! To save the time of spiralising the vegetables yourself, many supermarkets sell pre-spiralised and pre-mixed vegetables.

1   Top the wrap with all the ingredients.

2   Roll up and secure the wrap.

1 sun-dried tomato wrap

2 large handfuls of spiralised vegetables, such as carrot, beetroot (beet) and zucchini (courgette)

small handful of parsley

½ avocado, sliced

1 teaspoon toasted sesame seeds

Lemony tahini dressing
- 2 tablespoons tahini
- 1 tablespoon Greek yoghurt
- 1 tablespoon lemon juice
- ½ teaspoon minced garlic

# Smoked trout wrap

Smoked trout combines beautifully with the other ingredients in this wrap – but, if you prefer, you could swap it out with flaked, tinned tuna.

1   Top the wrap with all the ingredients.

2   Roll up and secure the wrap.

1 spinach wrap

75 g (2½ oz) smoked trout, flaked

1 hard-boiled egg, peeled and quartered

handful of watercress sprigs

½ avocado, sliced

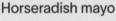

Horseradish mayo
- 2 tablespoons mayonnaise
- 1 teaspoon minced horseradish
- 1 teaspoon lemon zest

# Baked tofu & satay wrap

This crunchy, colourful wrap is simple to put together. To save time, make a few batches of the sauce ahead of time and store it in the fridge.

1  Mix the satay sauce ingredients together and season to taste.

2  Spread the satay sauce over the wrap.

3  Top with the remaining ingredients.

4  Roll up and secure the wrap.

1 tomato wrap

handful of shredded carrot

handful of shredded red cabbage

100 g (3½ oz) packaged baked tofu, sliced

¼ red bell pepper (capsicum), thinly sliced

handful of chopped roasted peanuts

Satay sauce
- 3 tablespoons peanut butter
- 2 tablespoons lime juice
- 1 tablespoon hoisin sauce
- 1 teaspoon maple syrup
- ½ teaspoon minced garlic

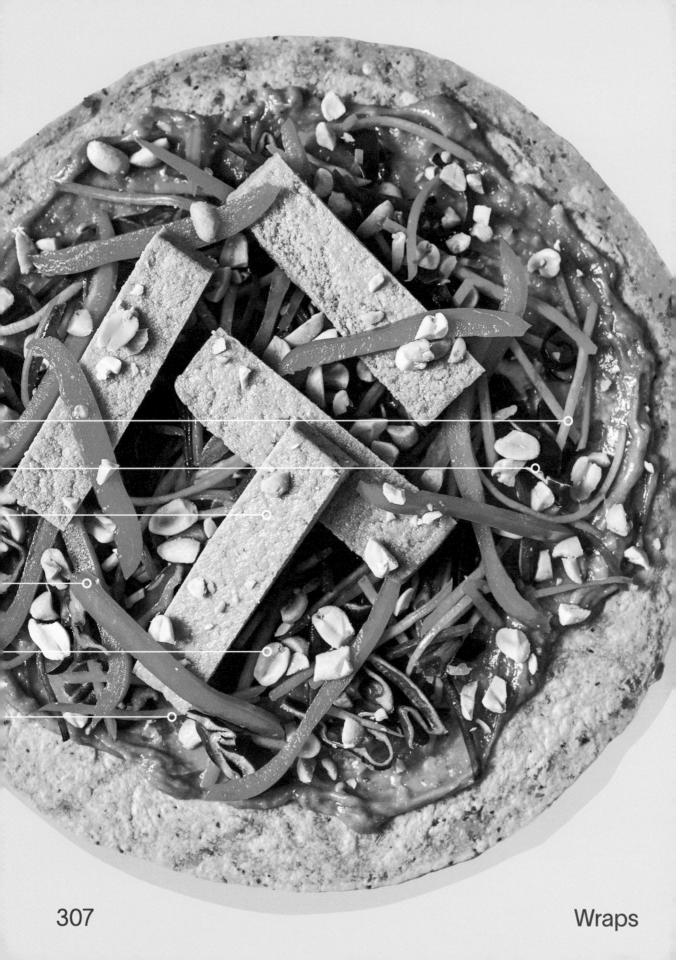

# Tricolour veggie wrap

This tasty wrap is a fresh take on the humble salad sandwich. If you like, make your own hummus in advance so you have this delicious spread ready to go at any time.

1  Spread the hummus over the wrap.

2  Top with the remaining ingredients.

3  Roll up and secure the wrap.

60 g (¼ cup) hummus

1 spinach wrap

small handful of alfalfa sprouts

handful of baby spinach leaves

¼ yellow bell pepper (capsicum), thinly sliced

1 tomato, sliced

1 short cucumber, halved lengthways and sliced

lemon juice, to taste

# Tomato & cashew cheese wrap

Cashew cheese is a delicious vegan spread that's full of flavour. You can usually find it in most supermarkets – but making your own is straightforward too!

1  Cook the spinach in boiling water for 30 seconds. Drain, cool, squeeze out any liquid and finely chop.

2  Mix the spinach with the remaining ingredients and season to taste.

3  Spread the mixture over the wrap.

4  Roll up and secure the wrap.

100 g (3½ oz) baby spinach leaves

100 g (3½ oz) cashew cheese

handful of cherry tomatoes, halved

¼ yellow bell pepper (capsicum), finely diced

¼ red onion, finely chopped

2 teaspoons lemon juice

1 spinach wrap

# Sweet potato & tahini wrap

Most left-over roast vegetables would work here, including pumpkin (winter squash) and potatoes. The tahini sauce is so versatile – it can be used in many different types of salads.

1 Mix the tahini sauce ingredients together.

2 Top the wrap with the cabbage, sweet potato and onion.

3 Pour the tahini sauce evenly over the top.

4 Roll up and secure the wrap.

1 wrap

handful of shredded red cabbage

200 g (7 oz) left-over roasted sweet potato, cut into chunks

¼ red onion, thinly sliced

Tahini sauce
- 2 tablespoons tahini
- juice of ½ lemon
- 1 teaspoon minced garlic
- 2 teaspoons water, plus extra if needed

# Mexican bean & corn wrap

This classic combination of black beans, corn and avocado with the spice of jalapeños is a powerhouse of flavours – and filling, too!

1. Spread the sour cream over the wrap.

2. Roughly mash the avocado and lime juice together.

3. Top the wrap with the spinach, beans, jalapeño and corn.

4. Dot the avocado mix over the top. Season with salt and pepper.

5. Roll up and secure the wrap.

50 g (1¾ oz) sour cream

1 wrap

½ avocado

2 teaspoons lime juice

handful of baby spinach leaves

100 g (3½ oz) drained tinned black beans

4–5 pickled jalapeño slices, finely chopped

75 g (2¾ oz) drained tinned sweet corn kernels

# BBQ tempeh wrap

Tempeh is a fermented soy bean product that originated in Indonesia. There are many different types to choose from, so feel free to experiment to find your favourite.

1   Mix the mayonnaise and liquid smoke together.

2   Combine the coleslaw and onion and mix through the smoky mayonnaise.

3   Top the wrap with the coleslaw.

4   Evenly scatter the tempeh over the top. Season with salt and pepper.

5   Roll up and secure the wrap.

3 tablespoons mayonnaise

5–6 drops of liquid smoke

handful of pre-cut coleslaw mix

¼ red onion, sliced

1 wrap

80 g (2¾ oz) packaged ready-to-eat BBQ tempeh, sliced

# Falafel wrap

To ensure this wrap is the tastiest, track down the best-quality falafel balls. Some commercial varieties can be quite dry, if that's the case in your wrap, you might want to increase the amount of hummus.

1. Spread the hummus over the wrap.
2. Top with the remaining ingredients and season to taste.
3. Roll up and secure the wrap.

60 g (¼ cup) hummus

1 wrap

handful of shredded iceberg lettuce

3 falafel balls, roughly crumbled

2 spring (green) onions, sliced

handful of parsley, chopped

small handful of pickled turnips

chilli sauce, to taste

318

# Vegan sausage sizzle wrap

This might not be the healthiest option out there – but we all need a little comfort food now and again! No two vegan sausages are the same, so find the most delicious variety to use in this wrap.

1 Cook the sausages in the oil in a frying pan over high heat for 3–4 minutes.

2 Top the wrap with the lettuce, sausages, cheddar and shallots. Drizzle with ketchup and mustard. Season with salt and pepper.

3 Roll up and secure the wrap.

3 vegan sausages

2 teaspoons oil

1 wrap

handful of shredded iceberg lettuce

handful of shredded vegan cheddar

1 tablespoon crispy-fried shallots

tomato ketchup, to taste

American mustard, to taste

Wraps

# Curried egg(less) salad wrap

This vegan alternative to the traditional curried egg sandwich is a tasty, filling wrap that will definitely leave you satisfied for lunch.

1   Cook the tofu and curry powder in the oil in a frying pan over high heat for 3–4 minutes.

2   Spread the mayonnaise over the wrap.

3   Top with the curried tofu, watercress and onion. Season with salt and pepper.

4   Roll up and secure the wrap.

200 g (7 oz) firm tofu, finely diced

1 teaspoon curry powder

1 tablespoon oil

2 tablespoons vegan mayonnaise

1 wrap

handful of watercress leaves

¼ red onion, thinly sliced

# Beetroot & walnut wrap

This wrap is packed full of flavour and nutrition. Choose beetroot packed in minimal sugar for a healthier option. Alternatively, roast your own and store it in the fridge ready to use at any time.

1 Spread the pesto and rocket over the wrap.

2 Top with the remaining ingredients.

3 Roll up and secure the wrap.

2 tablespoons pesto

handful of baby rocket (arugula) leaves

1 spinach wrap

1 short cucumber, sliced

2 cooked baby beetroot (beets), quartered

50 g (½ cup) toasted walnuts, roughly chopped

2 teaspoons extra virgin olive oil

1 teaspoon lemon juice

# Index

Index

Published in 2022 by Smith Street Books
Naarm (Melbourne) | Australia
smithstreetbooks.com

ISBN: 9781922754073

Publisher: Paul McNally
Editors: Katri Hilden & Hannah Koelmeyer
Designer: Murray Batten
Cover designer: George Saad
Layout: Heather Menzies, Studio31 Graphics
Photographer: Chris Middleton
Food stylist: Deborah Kaloper
Indexer: Helena Holmgren
Proofreader: Pam Dunne

Printed & bound in China by C&C Offset Printing Co., Ltd.

Book 219
10 9 8 7 6 5 4 3 2

Recipes in this book have previously appeared in *The 5-Minute Salad Lunchbox*,
*The 5-Minute Vegan Lunchbox* and *The 5-Minute 5-Ingredient Lunchbox*,
published by Smith Street Books in 2019, 2021 and 2021 respectively.